a Pinch of Posh

a Pinch of Posh

A BEGINNER'S GUIDE TO BEING CIVILISED

Mr & Mrs Laurence Llewelyn-Bowen

Collins

First published in 2006 by
Collins, an imprint of
HarperCollins*Publishers* Ltd.
77–85 Fulham Palace Road
London w6 8jb

The Collins website address is:
www.collins.co.uk

Collins is a registered trademark of HarperCollins*Publishers* Ltd.

09 08 07 06

9 8 7 6 5 4 3 2 1

A catalogue record for this book is available from the British Library.

Senior Commissioning Editor: Jenny Heller
Copy-editor: Sarah Day
Senior Editor: Lizzy Gray
Jacket Design: Emma Ewbank
Design: Wolfgang Homola
Proof-reader: Anne Rieley
Indexer: Geraldine Beare

ISBN-10: 0-00-723626-3
ISBN-13: 978-0-00-723626-8

Printed and bound by Clays Limited, St Ives

Contents

Introduction

Whatever is a Pinch of Posh? To the uninitiated, it may seem as though spending One's days in a giddy whirl of drive-by antiquing and figurative napkin-folding were the life of Riley, but Poshness is about so much more than simply being hit with the la-de-dah stick. The Posh aren't born; they're made, and making One's self Posh takes time, hard work and scaffolding.

There may well be those who wonder why being Posh is so important (after all, it is what inspired your desperately well-tailored authors to write this book). Well, the world today is a shiny place of aspiration and twenty-four-hour fulfilment. Anyone, no matter who they are, can walk off the street and buy a four-poster bed or an enormous horse box with a coat of arms emblazoned on the side. Accidents of birth, of class, fortune and position now count for nothing. But although people today lead lives that have never looked better, felt more comfortable or appeared to be so styled, are they really happy? Underneath the trappings, are they smiling? Are they fulfilled? Can they carry off wearing brown in town on a weekday?

The word 'Posh' has no real meaning. It dictates that where One is going is so very much more important than from where One has come. Posh is as Posh does, and for the truly Posh comes the ultimate reward: free with every *Posh* life comes the indescribably incandescent cavalcade that is civilisation. That said, One may have wondered where civilisation has gone. How can that which has taken over 2,000 years to refine and hone vanish in a single generation? (And has anyone checked down the back of the sofa?) But civilisation has gone nowhere. It is everywhere, all around, up and down but, like the better sort of orange squash,

it has been diluted. In the best traditions of children's party fairness, the thick syrup of civilisation has been watered down so that we all might have a sip.

LET GLAMOUR BE THY GUIDE

Coping with Class

Class is an awful thing, and it is, thank goodness, dying out. When One inadvertently discovers an acquaintance with a latent fondness for the particular class to which they think they belong, it's all terribly unpleasant to watch.

As a badge of allegiance, some people will even go out of their way to acquire particular possessions which declare their perceived class. The following is a useful observational checklist:

Upper-class trappings: A user's guide

THE SINISTER (AND DEXTER) WORLD OF HERALDRY – Over hundreds of years of top-level board meetings, the complications of the shield, the supporter, the motto, and the crest were created to keep all but the upper echelons of society at bay.

FAMILY PORTRAITS – The upper classes hang family portraits in chronological order, which serves to highlight how quickly gene pools run dry.

FAMILY SILVER – One may suggest to One's upper-class friends that obsolete silver items such as wig-curlers, crumb-brushes, grape-shears, bonnet-buffers or posset-syringes can be most successfully introduced into contemporary erotic practices.

LIVESTOCK – The upper classes love livestock more than anything. In fact, it has been conjectured that the upper classes love their livestock more than their own rather complicated families.

Lower-class trappings: The pot calling the vase Ming(ing)

PATTERNED CARPETS AND HORSE BRASSES – A theory exists that those who consider themselves lower class like the idea of living in a pub. The truth is that lower-class people once felt the lack of household staff very keenly, so they were naturally drawn to patterned carpet (particularly large, vaguely rococo-inspired volutes scattered across an incandescent red ground), because they needed little cleaning and are more fun to watch than television. Horse brasses, on the other hand, remain a mystery.

LIVESTOCK – People of lower-class proclivities prefer livestock of a different variety to that of the upper classes. Pigeons, greyhounds and aggressive-looking dogs are very popular.

LANDSCAPING, THE LADS' WAY – People who enjoy the anti-cultural sulkiness of the lower-class way (and this includes many aristocrats) like to use every spare piece of land as storage for large lumps of mechanical equipment which might be useful one day.

Can the Upper Classes Ever be Posh?

Ostensibly, the upper classes have all that's required to be as Posh as Posh can be: lovely things and not much money to get in the way. Unfortunately for them, however, there's nearly always a few niggling omissions or inadequacies which disqualify the majority of nobs from being truly Posh.

As a rule, the upper classes are still quixotically anchored to the bullying tactics of good manners and Correct Form, and they continue in their distressing tendency to believe themselves better than all others. But their real Achilles' heel is scruffiness, which, if left unchecked, may burgeon into fully-fledged under-grooming.

But, the above aside, there *are* shiny, lovely people of the upper classes who, thanks to great eccentricity, are marvellously Posh. They tend to occupy the very upper tier of upper classdom, yet are charming nonetheless. (So charming, in fact, that for a very chosen few, their scruffiness and slight tendencies towards malodorousness may be forgiven.)

By way of example of the upper-class Posh, may we offer the following shiny list:

* Dame Judi Dench (enchanting but can get a little spity if excited)
* The Dowager Duchess of Devonshire (the best Mitford of the bunch and, even in her 165th year, still very sexy)
* Lord Lucan
* Lord Tracey
* Tracey Lord
* Lord de Lord
* Lady Intimate-Complaint (pronounced 'Inthwit-Complatte')
* The Duchess of Northumberland (a woman so lovely grown men cry)
* The Duke of Earl-Earl-Earl-Duke-de-Earl KMG. VC. KC. VPQ
* Lord Attenborough of Middle Earth
* Lord McKellen of the Ring (not to be confused with Sir Ian McKellen)
* The Dowager Countess of Roundabout

Can the Lower Class Ever be Posh?

Most certainly, provided the commoner in question is prepared to abandon any tendencies towards aggressive sensitivity, sullen indignation or dancing with their thumbs in the invisible arm holes of imaginary waistcoats. True, the particular sulky inferiority that so blighted the lower classes was entirely caused by the sulky arrogance of the upper classes, but it's time now, please, to move on. It doesn't matter which class started it, let's now all address ourselves to becoming Posh together and let bygones be bygones.

Posh is as Posh does

Taking a Little Bit of Posh and Spreading it Ever so Thinly: Posh Trumps

As an informative exercise, a few celebrated names have been chosen at random for discussion. All are marked out of seventeen for Poshness:

HM The Queen – not conventionally Posh, as she is the figurehead of Correct Form and very difficult to accessorise, but saved from a very low mark by a jolly good sense of humour. Posh Rating: 9

HRH Sarah Duchess of York – handicapped at birth by being of gingerkind. Has recently been polished up like a pebble. Rotten laugh. Posh Rating: 7

Madonna – still lovely at seventy-two, and bendy with it. Looks good in tweed. Needs to work harder on being nice. Posh Rating: 15

Nicole Kidman – really something of a Posh icon. An exemplar of how the former colonies can produce some of the prettier Posh. Posh Rating: $13^8/9$

Sir Elton John – a good example of some One who loves lovely things but forgets to get any pleasure from them. Not Posh. Posh Rating: $6^4/9$

Hugh Grant – some very shiny bits. Charming his way out of being publicly humiliated proved to be something of a mouthful. Posh Rating: 13

The late Queen Victoria – far too grumpy to be Posh and rather foolishly preferred small, silly crowns. Posh Rating: 2

Pharaoh Akhenaton of Egypt – known for the greatest makeover in the history of Egypt. Married to the lovely Nefertiti (8 extra marks) and possibly Tutankhamen's dad (fabulous taste in bling). Posh Rating: 16

Jamie 'Pukka' Oliver – a tad over-bouncy and not at all easy on the eye. Let down by a 'must try harder' wardrobe. Lovely social conscience, however. Posh Rating: $4^1/16$

DONALD TRUMP – a non-starter due to the improbable hair.
   Posh Rating: 3
IVANA TRUMP – a non-starter due to the improbable hair.
   Posh Rating: 3
BATMAN – despite all the brooding, the *Poshest* and the chicest of all the
   superheroes. Also has a talented eye for interiors. *Posh* Rating: 12
THE LATE OSCAR WILDE – handicapped at birth by a very large face
   indeed. But, thanks to tailoring and a wit so sharp it cut without pain,
   a very respectable score. *Posh* Rating: $11^3/8$
THE LATE SIR CECIL BEATON – did more than any to give *Posh* a 'look',
   was a pioneer of the linguistic science of Bitchcraft and, by a bizarre twist
   of fate, the former owner of Madonna's current country seat, Ashcombe
   House in Dorset. *Posh* Rating: 15
DOLLY PARTON – is without question the very epitome of *Posh*. Lovely
   both inside and out, lustrous in the extreme and entirely at home in her
   own skin (of which she has a surprising amount and which is, to every last
   bit, marvellous). *Posh* Rating: $16^9/10$

So, dear reader, get set for a new methodology that sets out the good, the
bad and the ugly for a post-punk generation who find themselves, rather
startled, at the very top of the food chain. We need a new way of approaching civilisation, which takes the best of the old and the very loveliest of the
new. We need a social code that's accessible, affordable and shiny in the
extreme. We need a Pinch of *Posh*, and we need it right now. So, sit up
straight, find a saucer for that cup, and prepare to be *Poshed*!

CHAPTER ONE

One

The Rule of One

To prove just how simple and straightforward the *Posh* way of being is, the God of all *Posh* things invented the *Rule of One*. The *Rule of One* has a geometry of such awe-inspiring perfection that most human minds find it impossible to understand. And what humans don't understand, they so very often deride and despise. But more of man's inhumanity to One later.

This is the *Rule of One*:

If:
I am me, you are you, they are they

Then also:
I am One, you are One, they are One
We, all of us, are Ones together

The *Rule of One* is not just grammar or semantics. No, the *Rule of One* is about respect. The *Rule of One* puts me, you, they, us and we in exactly the same boat and therefore dictates respect for every One as a One in their own right. It's neither male nor female, singular nor plural, rich, poor, pretty, old or young. It's One, and as such is all inclusive, democratic and available to all, or indeed to every One.

But, these days, in our darkened world of knuckle-dragging reactionaries, use 'One' at your peril. 'One' has become, quite wrongly, a symbol of powerful hate and resentment akin to that towards a witch's third nipple, or indeed a festoon blind.

Why has the Rule of One fallen so decisively out of favour? For many, many centuries, it has not been in the interests of the initiated to share important information like how 'One' works. The smooth running of a feudal society depended entirely on class dictating who was in charge and who wasn't. After all, it's a difficult moment when One realises One's indoor staff are actually lovelier than One.

If the Rule of One is the mystical expression of the truth contained within the holy word 'Posh', then it's easy to see how the leaden brains of the terminally politically correct have been confused. The Rule of One and the Pursuit of Posh have been erroneously entombed in the cracked and crumbling sarcophagus marked 'class'. In fact, for many, the words 'Posh' and 'class' are stupidly, misguidedly synonymous. *Wrong*, so very, very, very *wrong*.

Class is wrong and bad and should be stamped out and stamped on until its pestilent venom oozes unchecked into the gutter. Class is snobbery, elitism and anything that elevates one person above another simply through accident of birth. One can't buy class, nor would One want to. There is nothing you can do with class: it's pointless. And as all those who have a class – upper, lower, middle or something somewhere in between – know, class is a dreary fact that has to be dragged to the grave. It can't be changed, improved or made-over, so the simple thing is to abolish it.

But what's to stop society spinning uncontrollably down the drain of bad behaviour and anti-civilisation? After all, the old class system did define what was 'good behaviour' and 'bad behaviour' and who One should look up to. Well, this is the crucial point, since this is where Posh takes over.

Posh has no particular class axe to grind, no hidden agenda (other than loveliness for all) and is exactly what our newly flattened society now needs. So, what exactly is *Posh*?

To be *Posh* is to be truly glamorous on the inside

To be *Posh* is to be the best One can be at being who One is. But more than that, it is to be the best One can be but also to be able to recognise the best every One else can be too.

Spotting a One (or indeed another One)

A One, a truly *Posh* One, will be easy to spot: shiny shoes, flawless skin, fragrant, bouncy hair, a lovely silky tail (if applicable) and an affable, approachable manner that oozes magnetism. One's clothes suit and flatter One's physique to Olympian perfection, conversation sparkles and flows like a waterfall designed by Mozart and One's smile makes the air reverberate every bit as movingly as that good bit from Emerson Lake and Palmer's 'Fanfare for the Common Man'.

And all of this is because that particular One has worked out exactly who they are, what they are, what they want and who they want to do it with. They're lovely because they're happy. And never forget that in the land of the blind the one-eyed man is king – behold the filth, degradation, unhappiness and overhead lighting that surround us; it's never been easier to be incandescently *Posh*, because never before has mankind been so deeply uncivilised and, indeed, quite so unhappy.

Poshture – the erect spine and open, gilded countenance of One who's so very at home with being One – is another obvious clue to spotting a One (for more on *Poshture* see page 32). There are also behavioural habits that give the game gloriously away. For example, the use of 'One' but not *overuse* of One. And of course there's the way that Ones treat other Ones. Some One really and truly *Posh*, some One who has attained a level of civilisation unheard of since the days of diamond-buckled knee breeches will do any-thing – up to and including death – to be both *interested in* and *interesting to* you.

Spotting a One in the dark

In the absence of the visual triggers of loveliness, the Posh are nevertheless easy to single out. Contemporary culture would call Posh 'high self-esteem', which is a horrid way of using a lovely word like 'esteem'. It has to be said that anything prefaced with the word 'self' is to be avoided – self-abuse, self-pollination, self-harm, self-service. No, the Posh simply have esteem. The Posh have esteem in buckets. And it's the sort of esteem that's not just kept for personal use but also passed around and shared by all. The Posh have so very much esteem it's contagious. Unfortunately, the uninitiated confuse this charming confidence with arrogance or narcissism, but that's just because they tend to be both ugly and crap.

Correct Form v. the Posh

Before Posh (BP) there was the Correct Form. It was what the upper classes used to protect themselves from change, from excitement, from anything new, interesting or sexy. From the Correct came etiquette, and from eti-quette came manners.

In the beginning, One has to admit, the majority of what is understood as manners were little laws and codes created to make the world run more smoothly and more prettily. But more smoothly and more prettily for whom? Correct Form established beyond doubt One's origins and whether One was upper, middle, lower or working class. It could not, of course, provide any sense of One having a destination beyond One's class. And that is the most important difference between the frigidity of Correct Form and the loveli-ness of Posh.

Posh is creatively energetic, it assimilates new and better ways of approaching old issues. It bends in the breeze to accommodate the winds of change. Correct Form remains static, fossilised by its own definitions of right and wrong, which is why the concept of Correct Form helped fan the flames of class war in the first place. Correct Form, good manners and etiquette quickly became despised symbols of subjugation through class. Understandable, yes, but dangerous in that no replacement was conceived to fill the void (rule number one of all successful revolutions). So every One started behaving very badly and selfishly indeed as a self-conscious statement of personal class warfare. And what a pointless thing that was. Still, thanks to our fabulous Authors' effulgent generosity, that's all in the past. From now on, it will be niceness that defines us, along with decently supportive under things, great teeth and a creatively original approach to napkin-folding.

Throwing Spanners at Good Manners

One of the key secrets of *Posh* is to take control. Wherever you are, whatever you are doing, fairly, firmly and fabulously rise like a champagne bubble to the surface of every situation. And to do this, it's more than essential to know One's enemy.

Now, your beloved Authors, their diaries being as they are, simply cannot justify to themselves the pointless regurgitation on the finer points of Correct Form or the churning out of pages and pages on manners. Far better, Dear Reader, would be to conduct exhaustive background reading on the subject on your own. There are very, very, very many books written by elderly and/or irrelevant authors on manners, and a short afternoon scanning their vapid 'do's and don'ts' will be enough to give One a good grounding in their pointless ways and also, incidentally, give One a migraine, a dizzy compulsion to smoke cigarettes before the loyal toast and a misplaced desire to wear brown shoes with a blue suit.

The only thing One must remember is that the most perfect manners are only achieved when One breaks the rules. But never break rules with a sledgehammer. Break the rules of good manners in the way that Mozart broke the rules of harmony or, indeed, in the way that Frank Zappa broke the rules of facial hair (and harmony).

*Throw spanners
at good manners*

Makeshift Manners Maketh Man

Fundamentally, One will always get manners 'right' if One is nice. Anything else – raising One's hat to a lady, standing when an elder enters a room, tapping the end of One's codpiece with a three-quarter-folded fan – is all just icing on the cake of niceness (although tapping some One else's codpiece with a three-quarter-folded fan should be seen more as an invitation).

Interestingly, however, when it comes to lubricating the friction that can develop between the sexes, rigid good manners of the old-school variety becomes a fascinatingly effective tool. But then, mating these days relies more and more on effective tools.

The traditional definition of gentility – 'a gentleman is someone who is never *knowingly* rude' – makes an important point. Unintentional rudeness is, if nothing else, a missed opportunity. Do see page 75 for guidance on swearing with style.

If unintentional rudeness is wrong, is intentional politeness right?

There is nothing more patronising than text-book manners. When, in an exclusive shop or expensive restaurant, One gets oleaginously basted with Correct Form, peppered with 'Madams' and 'Sirs' and garnished with obsequiously wrung hands, One knows there's an attempt to put One in One's place. (One also knows One is also about to be charged for the dubious privilege.) Extreme manners are an act of social aggression and dirty play. They're about establishing dominance in order to create a moral high ground by illustrating a higher knowledge of good manners.

The Gentlemanly way ahead: Genticity

In olden times, society was composed thusly: Monarchy, Aristocracy, Squirachy, Gentility, Peasantry. The idea was that the vast majority, the Gentility, should be the nicest, because if they weren't, then either they'd be demoted to Peasantry or, worse still, they'd never achieve promotion to Squirachy, which came with a lovely shiny coat of arms.

So, Gentility became synonymous with niceness. Unfortunately, it also has become synonymous with lace curtains, crocheted antimacassars and china ornaments. Thus, to help revivify the concept of solid, middle-class good manners for all, our fabulous Authors propose that henceforth 'Gentility' be known as 'Genticity'.

The Million-Guinea Question: Is being British essential to being a One?

For the old guard, civilisation was British. It was in British power to devolve on nations lucky enough to find themselves subjugated by the Imperial British boot, but it was a one-way street with a non-return valve of prejudice ensuring there was absolutely no cultural blow-back. For the Correctists, Correct Form was 'British Form' and any other way of doing anything was wrong.

But then, that's because the British forget that there's a world of difference between the British and the English. Great Britain doesn't mean that Britain's *great*, it means that it is *greater*, in that it encompasses more than a handful of regions and each of those regions boasts its own flavour of people. Plus, of course, like the Romans 2,000 years before, membership of the British Brigade has been successfully and creatively extended to the best of the rest from all over the globe. If there's anyone having a moan about this, then they'll tend to be English (one of the larger British minorities), prone to freckling and complaining about the weather.

Posh, of course, dictates that this is all tosh. *Posh* is non-denominational, non-sectarian, non-racist and non-stick. The whole point about being a One is to value all other Ones as One values One's self, so if Ones from overseas have a particular way of being civilised that appeals, then *Posh* allows immediate absorption. In fact, keeping a deliberately open mind and maintaining a sponge-like state will ensure One's own Oneage remains vibrant, relevant and unique.

A Wonderful Conclusion

The point at which *Poshness* and politeness diverge is the point at which a human ceases to be merely human and starts to be divine. A parrot can be polite. Computers are polite. Even elevators tell One in polite ways at which floor One has arrived. But none of the above can be *Posh*.

Posh can't be learned like a dance step, a national anthem or the French technique for the exquisite fellation of a gentleman friend whilst whistling. No, it needs a spin to it, some home-grown creativity that gives in some areas and takes in others.

The point of *Poshness* is the confident ability to make politeness personal. Manners need to be seen as an engagingly old-fashioned recipe which relied on obsolete ingredients like class feudalism and suet for its effect. All a bit dotty and irrelevant. A bit like Grandma Walton, really.

And now, since it has been so exquisitely established that to be *Posh* is to be as glamorous on the inside as One is on the outside – exactly how lovely is your outside?

CHAPTER TWO

One's Presentation

Facing the World with a Flourish

Presenting One's self to a waiting planet is not just about tailoring (although that's 90 per cent of the battle won). A lovely-looking person is a walking advert for a lovely-looking personality, while a complete scruff obviously feels themselves simply to be not worth dressing nicely. How One presents One's self says everything about how One feels about One's self, and perfect presentation starts in the bathroom.

Toilette, Toilet and the Towelette

There simply are no excuses ever, ever, ever, for a human to smell like a beast. It will forever be indefensible. Loveliness, *Poshness* and being one of the great Ones will in perpetuity elude those who are not easy on the nose. Body odour is one of the single most common personal-space invasions in the world today. There is categorically nothing healthy in the smell of sweat and absolutely nothing sexy in the stench of hot bollocks, no matter what the Sportistic say.

But this is all very difficult to explain to a lot of humans, because they seem to furtively enjoy their own aroma and the way remote bits of them smell. Presumably, it has something to do with recognition and scent-marking, but this is the preserve of incontinent, deaf, dumb and blind street dogs. Perhaps it's to reassure themselves they are still there. Whatever the underlying reason, a warm furtive finger lingering too close to the nose when no One appears to be looking is suspicious at the very least. And at its worst, French.

Enjoy, if you must, the smell of One's person in the private comfort of One's own darkened habitation, but be sure to hang an easy-to-read sign on an external door so the rest of the world doesn't inadvertently intrude.

What is a Posh Wash?

Taking showers is fine if One is entirely at home with the sight of the naked body standing proud and shiny.

Baths have an advantage over showers in that there's no gravity in the tub, thus allowing water to circulate beneath any pendant areas of flesh One may be cultivating. Also, bubbles or any other murk-inducing agent may be introduced into the water to make it opaque. This means the majority of One's body remains tactfully veiled, apart from the longest and most pendulous bits (and therefore the most buoyant bits) which break the meniscus and float on the surface like fleshy lily pads.

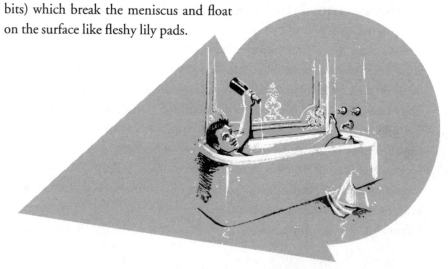

Scents and sensibilities: Why patchouli will never be Posh

Correct Form required perfume to be known as 'scent', which seems odd, given the word 'scent' is so often followed by the word 'gland'. Supposedly, 'perfume' (from the effetely French *parfum*) was too exotic and 'eau de cologne' ridiculous, for who would want to smell German? And as for the concept of 'eau de toilette' ...

Correct Form also dictated that One should be sparing to the point of minimalism when applying scent. This seems justified if the scent One is applying doesn't smell nice but is less than justifiable if, as One would expect, the scent smells of lovely, soft, musky cherubs tickling the inside of the nasal passage with their angora underpants.

Of course, don't overdo it. That is every bit an invasion of the personal space of others as pits that smell of pasty. Choose well and wisely. Select a *parfum* that is exactly what One would distil from One's glands if One had a choice in the matter.

Smells and what they say about One

PATCHOULI is favoured by the unclean, spiritualists and nymphomaniacs, as it covers One's tracks so vigorously.

MUSK is preferred by rats, love rats, Italian waiters (who produce their own musk from customised glands) and taxi drivers, all of whom think it attractive but few of whom have friends.

LILY OF THE VALLEY often rises in powdery clouds from old women who assume they are clean, which they may very well not be.

LAVENDER is favoured by poisoners and Ancient Romans but really doesn't smell that nice.

CEDAR scents once denoted 'Gentleman'; nowadays denotes 'tree-hugger'.

CORIANDER is best left to dress chickens.

Poshture

Gravity is a cruel and unforgiving concept which really should never have been invented. The way One looks and, more importantly, the way One looks One's best, may involve all sorts of interventions – medical, mechanical or electrical – but without Poshture, everything else is a waste of time. Poshture is the only thing in one's charmoury of loveliness that delivers a vigorous resistance to the wholesale invasion by the forces of gravity.

Even the longest breasts rise a fraction of an inch when One's shoulders are pulled proudly back; even a neck ingrained with wrinkles etched as deep as those of a flaccid scrotal sack can firm when One raises One's chin; and legs as stumpy as Dutch furniture may achieve a degree of grace simply by extending One's toes.

Can the Ugly Ever be Posh?

Only if they try very, very hard, keep to the shadows and wear nothing that might draw attention to themselves.

Can the Pretty Ever be Posh?

To a certain extent, life really couldn't be harder for the pretty. For a start, like all minorities out in public, people really will stare so. Then there's the heightened expectation that comes as a natural reaction to external loveliness – is what's inside as stupendous? For, of course, the basic tenet of Posh really does, inflexibly, dictate that One has to be as glamorous on the inside as One is on the outside, and if the external beauty bar is raised too high, there's no chance of the poor, over-stretched personality being able to compete.

No, technically speaking, it is really quite difficult for the pretty to be
Posh, in many cases simply because they erroneously feel that natural
beauty cannot be bettered, which is wrong, wrong, very wrong. Far better, in
fact, to be middling pretty but beautifully presented and kind and display an
extremely clever application of loveliness and great shoes.

Grooming: Buffing One's Self Up to a Wonderful Shine

Grooming is a very, very Posh thing indeed. Homosexualists often
claim grooming as their own but, in fact, grooming was Posh before homosexuability became fashionable. And, don't forget, homosexuability and
Poshness are not by any means incompatible (see Chapter 8, One's
Reproduction: Doing Sex).

Grooming allows One the marvellous opportunity of stroking One's self
for the positive benefit of One and all who look upon One. So much of the
grooming process should be seen as an opportunity to show every last
extremity how highly it is valued; to treat it to serious clipping, descaling and
declagging, followed by a couple of coats of a lustrous varnish. And, indeed,
it should be each and every One's responsibility to look, at all times, entirely
fuckulent. Anyone can be clean but only the truly Posh are groomed.

The do's and don't's of grooming

The old way of Correct Form stated unequivocally that gentlefolk under-
groom as a matter of pride. Let it be known now that under-groomers are
bullies. Being seen in public by others in an under-groomed state suggests a
snarling disregard for the aesthetic sensibilities of the world around One, and
a bombastic selfishness that cannot be easily forgiven.

If the most important 'Do' of grooming is 'Do Do it', then the most important 'Don't' is 'Don't Do it in public'. This is for several reasons. Number one: the procedures involved in grooming (as well as a lot of the equipment) are of a very personal nature and are often best achieved without clothes. Number two: the concept of 'A dandy's handy but a fop's a flop' (see page 43) should be respected, in that the groomed state in which you first greet the world outside should be designed as the successful state in which to spend the day. Only fops fiddle with their finished effect; dandies do it well enough in the first place. (Besides, the effect One is left with having applied lipstick whilst travelling on a bus at 30 mph over speed humps is less like making-up and more like colouring-in.)

Glamoflage: Marvellous, marvellous maquillage

The 'natural look' was almost certainly invented by One of those aggressively ugly fashion journalists who decided in their bitterness that, if they couldn't be attractive, then neither should One.

Like depilation, make-up has an ancient history rich with the symbolism of civilisation. Its traditions enshrine the laws of Posh across many cultures and allow the human fully to achieve an aesthetic potential way beyond the base unmade-up state. There is no upper limit on make-up, do what thou wilt to make thy face up, even if it means sanding between coats and a lightly tinted shellac at the end of it.

The only mistake to be made with make-up is lighting. It's common sense, really, that if One is made up like an extraordinarily attractive Egyptian mummy, all heavy eyeliner and bituminous foundation, One should avoid well-lit areas like public transport, libraries, offices or doctor's waiting rooms. No, as the lovely people of the past knew well, wallow in the loveliness of half-light – the theatre, a heavily draped gondola or most concrete under-passes. Also avoid reflective surfaces (a tip your Augustan Authors are pleased to credit to their machine-washable friend Ms Joan Collins).

Should One be in any doubt, here is a checklist for foolproof grooming.

$\mathcal{D}$o	$\mathcal{D}$on't
Apply make-up with an air compressed spray gun	Paint One's teeth with water based paint
Count One's self lucky God invented conditioner	Dismiss beauty spots
Make sure there's always a back-light	Stand too close to a radiator in full make-up
Exfoliate	Expectorate
Embrace the mystical powers of vertical stripes	Be seduced by the honeyed words of a personal shopper with a vicious hangover
Plunder the past for inspiration	Emulate any One or any Thing that wandered hooded through the Middle Ages with a hand bell
Treat yourself to an occasional going-over with good-quality furniture polish	Substitute a stout vacuuming for a thoroughly soapy wash
Turn your back on dry shampoo	Inhale Shake'n'Vac
Take time to enjoy what's reflected in the mirror	Forget every One else sees it the other way around
Feel free to spend every last penny One owns on looking lovely	Dress to repress
Buy rose-tinted glasses for every One One's likely to meet	Ever look, smell or taste like cheese

Downstairs Grooming

What One does to One's own private self has a surprising bearing on how One feels.

'COLLARS AND CUFFS' was once an obsessive mantra for the bottle blonde. But, as with successful interior decoration, an eclectic combination above and below can create a warm welcoming atmosphere and, besides ...

PRUNING THE LAWN OF LOVE has become so ubiquitous that anyone making a call to One's downstairs is unlikely to find a shred of evidence that One's upstairs hair colour is not One's own

DARING DEPILATION has long been a universal indicator of civilisation. The removal of the animalistic pelt is a symbolic but also practical denial of One's simian origins. It encourages air flow and gives un-fragrant bacteria little to cling to. Indeed, when One looks back to the 1970s, the sight of a gentleman's torso flocked in oily, curled hair and the bizarre appearance of a lady with a quite endless triangle of shrubbery linking her navel to her inner thigh can't help but cause a giggle.

TATTOOS (whether downstairs or upstairs) are flawed on two levels. Firstly, the drawing is often unaccomplished (there are of course exceptions although, generally speaking, in our world, the standard of drawing is always regrettably unaccomplished). Secondly, the colours achieved are all hideous. Should One wish to embellish the base of the spine with a crudely drawn and turgidly coloured motif, does it really have to be permanent? Not to mention the eternal humiliation of misspellings.

PIERCING THINGS TO KEEP JEWELLERY IN makes sense if One is prone to losing things.

THE ACHILLES' HEEL OF GROOMING – TOES AND FEET The least lovely extremity is the foot. Poor feet – not only are they horribly difficult to draw, they are never really very nice to look at. So, as with fat, ugly people, ensure your feet don't offend by being poorly groomed, badly washed or generally on show in public.

Hair Crimes and Comb-Overs

Unlike the face, the hair profits from less cosmetic intrusion. It's simply nice when it's shiny and inviting to the touch. But, there is nothing that has profited more from the extraordinary advances in science and technology than hair care.

The fact that One might Teflon-coat One's 'do in this day and age demonstrates so clearly why the human race is at the very top of the food chain. Even ornate coiffures may be created with hair that looks like *hair* rather than the thigh fur of an unloved street dromedary. (Or, indeed, Tom Selleck's chest pelt.) No, nowadays, high hair needn't be self-harm hair.

Since One is looking back and picking the scab that was the bad old days of back-combing – spare a cackle for comb-overs. If nothing else, the oily traducement of hair from one region of the head over to another, unpopulated area, is an ugly, unconvincing euphemism. It tries to assert that, rather than being *largely* bald, the bearer is only *semi*-bald, which really is no better. Any One Posh knows that losing One's hair creates a perfect opportunity to either buy some lovely wigs or to burnish One's gloriously unhairy head to a rich, lustrous shine.

Overwear, an Overview

As this journey through the ravishing, rolling landscapes of *Posh* continues, it becomes more than apparent that One's clothes say more about One than words ever can. This truth is handy beyond belief, once learned. For with this immutable statement ever in One's mind as One's wardrobe for the week ahead is pondered upon, One will inescapably be inspired to 'Dress for Success'. And once the perfect selection is made, the celestial balance of beauty *within* and beauty *without* is achieved.

The real secret is utterly and entirely to ignore One's context. Rather than dressing warmly in endangered fur in the Arctic or in cool cotton for the tropics, formally for a drinks party at the Palace or in relaxed, horizontal stripes for yachting, *dress how thou wilt*. Indeed, really, it's only polite to show the world who One truly is by the clothes One chooses. Feel free to pick an angry palette of reds and oranges during that difficult time of the month. Soft white feather wings with a silver-sequined kaftan will show One's colleagues that One is very much at peace with One's self. A professional, hard-working demeanour accessorised by a high ponytail, unironed socks and a discrete sprinkling of pustules will get any One through a tricky exam. However, a lace jabot, rustling knee breeches and a PVC mac will indicate to all that One's taste for the popular music of the 1980s is having a fatal effect on One's wardrobe and must be stopped.

Dress instead to suit One's mood, suit One's predilections, suit who One feels One is to be that day. Never ever dress to be appropriate or to fit in or to be noticed. Dress to be One.

That said, there are some looks more difficult successfully to occupy than others:

HISTORICALLY ACCURATE COSTUME with archeologically exact
  underwear and a million fiddly fastenings really does need a lot of living
  up to. If attempted, steer clear of historical tourist attractions, or else
  visiting Americans will offer money to be photographed by One's side.

Clothing made from unusual materials, such as marine plywood, glass or chocolate never really caught on for reasons of practicality. One needs phenomenal reserves of *Posh* to enjoy wearing a wooden blouse ... not to mention the frightful splinters.

Armour, since made of metal sheets, also suffers the above disadvantages (minus the splinters) – although being partially armoured is very, very sexy.

Mutton dressed as Spam has to be the most difficult look to pull off effectively. Few of a certain age can feel comfortable exposing blue-cheese-marbled naked upper thighs beneath the smallest of micro-minis. And sequined boob tubes barely containing the long thin strips that were once boobs to be tubed rarely make One feel good about One's self.

Anything emblazoned with the name of its maker or manufacturer leads One to conclude that money has changed hands in return for advertising the garment in question. Should One actually wish to be seen as a walking billboard, then labels scattered thickly about One's person as if One were a Grand Prix driver can only be seen as a good thing.

Smasual Clothing (as in smart-casual) is horribly contrived. Following extensive practice, One may attempt draping knitwear over the shoulders and tying it in a knot at the chest. This look requires ruffled hair, a self-knowing smirk, and Spanish blood.

National Dress can be very seductive, particularly if it involves a wealth of gaily coloured ribbons. Be warned, it's a hard habit to quit.

Sportswear (see Sportswear, page 48)

Wear-and-Tear Wear (see Wear-and-Tear Wear, page 48)

Bare Wear rather defeats the point of all of those thousands of years of civilisation. Frankly, naturism is hard to comprehend and has a disastrous effect on the more fleshy extremities, which become used to not being supported and surrender themselves unquestionably to gravity as a result.

Tailoring: A gift from the gods

Of all the weapons of loveliness One can deploy from the charmoury, tailoring is the sharpest and the deadliest. The ability to take anything from fur pelts to lengths of plasticised, William Morris-inspired chintz and shape it to the body is akin to the original act of creation.

Indeed, forget not, that the first thing Adam and Eve did after eating the apple of knowledge from the brainy tree was get dressed. Getting dressed goes further than simply hiding One's shame (in fact, there's a degree of fun to be had in discreetly drawing attention to One's shame). Clothes give every One an ability to advertise a personality, express a view or generally catch the eye without a word being spoken.

The invention of the seams on which tailoring depends marked a critical moment in the evolution of civilisation. So it is with a heavy heart that One remarks on how few seams One sees on our streets today. The ridiculous enthusiasm for sportswear and the misguided lust for 'comfort' ensure that most people today wear almost entirely seam-free baby clothes created on a giant scale in childish colours and easycare fabrics (see Sportswear on the morbidly obese, page 48).

To be 'in tailoring' is to be at One's best. Ladies should accentuate their small waists, elegantly extend their shoulders, lengthen their legs and exquisitely part and dart their breasts. Yum. Gentlemen have the exquisite opportunity to become a steep inverse triangle with a shoulder line of Michelangelo-esque perfection, sumptuously tapering calves, a taut barrel of a chest and a trouser package of discreet enormity. Never mind the failing flesh beneath, the slouches' pouches, loose garlands of skin, flaccid puckerings and extremities withered to the size of *vol-au-vent* cases.

Through the humble tailor, the God of the Ancient Greeks speaks: man can, and must, strive to be a God. And a Posh God at that.

Arranging One's Self:
(the art of genital genticity)

To say it is of paramount importance that One's person does not break the line of One's tailoring would be an understatement of pointless proportions. This is why earlier ages, such as the Renaissance, created comforting cantilevered structures in which a gentleman could store his tenderest attachments, and a lady's errant upper thighs were politely draped by heavy skirts hung from converted cartwheels. This ensured that clothes were people-shaped, which is far better than the modern preoccupation to make people clothes-shaped.

These days, Posh dictates a reasonable and civilised attitude to the support and constraint of One's fleshier possessions, acknowledging their existence but giving little idea of their true shape. One doesn't need a 'perfect body' to be Posh – in fact, spending too much time and too much effort on the shape of the naked body seems Oneanistic (unless, of course, One hires One's naked body out for pleasure and or profit – see Mixing Business with Pleasure, page 90). No, Posh is about making do with what One has got, and that requires decent, honest, hardworking under-things.

Avoiding discomfort: Gentlemen
The reason One's tailor enquires 'to which side One dresses' is to ensure the top of his tape measure meets nothing during its ascent of the gentleman's inner thigh. The answer few tailors like to hear is that neither the right side nor the left side is occupied but that One's person is set at magnetic north.

Since the male has a natural bias towards the left or to the right (marking a centre line is called priapism and should either be medically treated or pro-fessionally exhibited), the advice of a valet or handyman with a spirit level should be sought to ascertain One's very own erogenous *comfort* zone.

Avoiding discomfort: Madam's upstairs

For ladies, the extremes of temperature in spring encourage the hasty removal of knitwear or outer tailoring, which occasions the off-putting but seasonal sight of 'hot cross baps'. Scooping One's self into a too small or too slack bra simply in the belief that it will have no effect on the line of an outer garment brings with it the urgent responsibility of not removing that outer garment. No matter how sunny it gets.

Avoiding discomfort : Madam's downstairs (or, reordering my lady's chamber)

For some unknown reason, there are ladies who believe unequivocally that the fuller the front of their trousers, the better. The resultant bulge (similar to a de-shelled oyster riding astride the blade of a paper knife) has many non-complimentary names.

Should One's lady person be prone to forming an intimate internal attraction to the centre seam of a trouser gusset, a strip of yoghurt pot cut to a comfortable length will be enough to separate the embarrassing intimacies. (Thanks, by the way, to the National Federation of Personal Shoppers for this tip.)

Rearranging in public

Rearranging One's make-up, One's hair, One's lapel or One's teeth in public is bad enough, since it smacks of foppishity. But to rearrange One's person, twang One's bra strap, 'head One's gusset off at the pass' or 'use the cue ball to kiss the pink back into the pocket' are soon to be made a capital offence. No judge. No jury. Just immediate lethal injection. And should the miscreant have covertly dragged a sly finger under their nose following rearrangement, then the lethal injection will be administered using the flat back of a coal shovel.

A Dandy's Handy but a Fop's a Flop

The Posh have been known by many names (some not so very nice), which allude to their quest for loveliness: Macaronis, Incroyables, Bright Young Things, 'It' girls, Coxcombs, Swells and New Romantics are but a few, but the terms 'Dandy' and 'Fop' are the ones that survive.

Fops don't dress for loveliness, they dress to create a fuss, to draw attention to their over-preening and bolster their easily wilted self-esteem. Each reflective surface they pass will cause a flutter of self-preening and picking. They do not dress for themselves, they dress for others.

Dandies plan their dress, enjoy the ritual of selection and relish the detail. The toilette of a Dandy is lengthy, the steps required for loveliness complicated and tiring. But, once satisfied with the effect, the Dandy greets the day and *that is it*. Done and dusted. A pact has been made between the Dandy and their wardrobe and that codicil will not be broken until bedtime. Dandies very much dress for themselves, which means that they are never, ever out of place, never uncomfortable, neither under-dressed nor over-dressed, but always, always, unfailingly lovely. And that loveliness has no choice but rub off on all around.

Fending Off Fads

It really is terribly important to stick to One's guns when it comes to dress. When One has finally evolved a 'look' which flatters, reflects One's personality and glows with an irresistible loveliness, through lengthy trial and error, *change it not*. The world of fashion is an economy like any other, constructed to separate every One from One's money. The fashion industry does this by reinventing the wheel every season, and often several times in between. Fads were invented to mock Fops. They are jokes not to be taken seriously. They are never to be worn in public.

No, the Posh way is to stick with a basic block or outline and, then, with a considered eye, introduce a gaily coloured nosegay or bangle in a fashionable hue, just to show the rest of the race how it's done.

Never dress to fit in

Fashion/Fad	Date	What it said about One
Oxford Bags	1930s	One had so very much to keep in One's trousers, One's trousers needed to be huge.
Puffball Skirts	Early 1980s & today	Having a bum at the front as well as the back seemed a good idea at the time, honest.
Round Hose	1560s–1600s	The male puffball. A large pair of pink satin spheres either side of a proudly protruding codpiece sent out a specific and not very subtle message.
Muffs	1300s–now	A marvellous place to put idle fingers.
Having One's bottom two ribs removed	1950s–now	Makes One bendy, and makes One's waist measure less than One's neck.
Shoulder Pads	1940s & 1980s	A useful fashion for the pear-shaped, turning them instead into the tea-chest-shaped.
Ceruse	Time immemorial until 1790s	Whitening One's face with poisonous lead pigments started the vogue for suicide blonding.
Leggings	For men, the Middle Ages; for women, the 1980s & the Middle Aged	Perfect for the frigid, since they guarantee the wearer will never, ever inspire ardour in anything with a heartbeat.
Crochet	Late 1960s	Useful for exhibitionists who like to expose themselves in small hexagonal instalments.
The Natural Look	1990s	Or the 'can't be bothered to look in any way nice' look, as it should be known.

Underwear: Making silk purses for spaniel ears

There are moments, One has to admit, when specialist or exotic under-things have a job to do. But what must be understood is that that very job presupposes that no outer clothes are to be required. In fact, to go further, specialist or exotic underclothes create far more problems than they solve (see Arranging One's Self – the art of genital genticity, page 41).

Just as a good, stout weatherproof undercoat is required for the final glossy topcoat when painting One's front door, underwear for daily wear should be practical and offer a solid foundation. Indeed, like decorating, successful dressing is all in the preparation.

Decent underwear should feel like the tough-love touch of a sensitive nanny, but please don't feel it need be unsexy. Practicality and eroticism often go hand in hand. Don't forget, a starchy cupping from a starchy nanny has helped many a young gentleman along the road to manhood (Lord Byron being one).

But for some absolutely inexplicable reason, the shape-changing potential long associated with underwear has fallen into decline. Bad shapes notwith-standing, what about the positive benefits of owning bosoms like intergalactic nose cones? Or a waist so small that one sneeze would snap it? Or a trouser proportion inspired by the florid art of the mid-Victorian sofa upholsterer? Ages past had huge fun playing games with the proportions of their bodies. There are plenty of gentlemen today who would love to see bottoms revived to the scale of their crinoline-wearing great-great-grand-mothers. Oh yes indeed.

What One's underwear says about One

A STRING VEST – a pigeon-keeping loner who lives on the roof

A JOGGING BRA – some One embarrassed about their amplitude but unable to find the time to exercise

LARGE Y-FRONTS WITH A BACK BESMIRCHMENT – a gentleman negligent at his toilette; almost certainly plays rugby at the weekend

FOX-FUR BRIEFS – a tickle addict

POP SOCKS – either the wearer is Japanese or a cross dresser into 'dowdy'

WHALE-BONE CORSETING – a thoroughly lovely One of more largessage than most

A THONG – indicates some One who will spend the rest of the day squirming

A THONG ON BACK TO FRONT – indicates some One who will spend the rest of the day with a secret smile

A PADDED BRA – a jolly sensible arrangement for the less ample. Not a good look on gentlemen

SPLIT CROTCH BRIEFS – an escape artist frightened of commitment

NOTHING WHATSOEVER – a commando or a pigeon-keeping loner who lives on the roof

Exotic underthings only create more problems than they solve

Other Kinds of Wear

Sportswear

Up until the twentieth century, sportswear was really just an ever so slightly relaxed version of ordinary lovely wear. This proved to have a very civilising influence on the game being pursued by the sportists.

Today, loutish sportswear encourages loutish sports and, to make matters worse, the loutish sportswear has now inexplicably escaped on to our streets.

Sportswear on the morbidly obese

Sportswear on the morbidly obese has to be the fifth horseman of the Apocalypse in seam-free, drip-dry disguise.

If it weren't so gut-churningly revolting, it could (as coffin humour goes) be rather amusing to watch the morbidly obese in their sportswear actually *do* sport. For added amusement, they could smoke a lot whilst they do it.

Wear-and-tear wear

Work wear, job wear, overalls, dungarees, aprons, pinnies and denim in general: it's all antithetical to Posh. But, that said, the clever can make even denim work for them provided it's worn with confidence, a broad smile and a voluptuous, almost bottomless bottom cleavage.

Countrywear: Why tweed is so very lovely

Before the invention of America, from which most wear-and-tear wear originates, every One wore tweed, which is tough, thorn-proof, practical, lovely to look at and allows One's personal moistness to escape unchecked through its attractive weft.

Tweed is lovely because, in the words of poet Rupert Brooke, it offers 'the rough male kiss of blankets' along with a soft mossiness, which ensures the tweed wearer is in a near constant state of arousal.

Tweed takes tailoring particularly well and thrives when seamed and seamed again. The soft shades of vegetable-dyed checks flatter any and every complexion. Further, the former rule of 'never wear brown in town' can be subverted on Fridays and Mondays by deliberately wearing tweed with brown leather accessories as a protest at having to work on days formerly spent at One's country retreat, retreating, relaxing and corridor-creeping.

But tweed has a dark side – in fact, a very dark side indeed: tartan. Tartan, when worn with something of a punky flourish, is at its most acceptable, but never ever wear tartan without a sense of humour – always keep the 'tart' in tartan.

Swimwear (all too often, too little, too late)

Swimming in public is a recent thing. The Victorians are, by and large, to be detested, but their ingenuity when it came to the origination of the roll-on, roll-off bathing machine should be grudgingly commended. But society moves on. The bathing-costume industry is now run by a panel of perverted myopics who actively seek to promote the irresponsible sale of lycra by the square centimetre to those on whom lycra should never be seen. Like so much that went wrong at the end of the twentieth century, minimalism, when applied to swimming things, marked a very, very low point in the history of civilisation. In fact, loosely fleshed middle-aged people bound tight with a few hastily tied strings and perhaps a microscopic pouch are somehow worse even than naturism (or Bare Wear). Pouring a quart of cellulite into a man-made-fibre pint pot is, One supposes, one way of keeping the flies off the ice cream.

The solution is not to fiddle with the design of the bathing suit itself but to invest in a series of draperies or flowing garments that can be tactfully worn over the never-flattering costume when not immersed in water.

What Not to Wear, Wear

Clothes that attract attention from the wrong sort (a bad thing)

These include:

* Bungee-jump décolletages
* Over-full cycling shorts
* Dungarees with a lot of *Dung* and little *Ree*
* Fur tippets with the preserved genitals of the fur-bearing animal concerned attached and in use as a decorative but rather fiddly clasp
* Sporrans with a hole in the back worn with a peep-front kilt
* Kilts
* Hats on the terminally self-conscious
* Full ripe man-breasts in tight lycra turtlenecks
* Inflatable couture

Clothes that attract attention from the wrong sort (a good thing)

These include:

* Lace underwear with One's price list elegantly embroidered on the gusset
* Pinstripe suits of such devilishly complex tailoring only one pinstripe is ever visible at any given moment
* Cufflinks with concealed eighteenth-century-porcelain perfume burners
* Fur coats with no knickers (ever)
* Motorised crinolines with concealed tractor seats (available in both manual and automatic)
* Surgical gloves
* Rose-tinted cling film (very flattering)
* Ruritanian cavalry uniforms with edible epaulettes
* Any Vivienne Westwood couture (take One's pick)
* Thigh-high waders

Tomfoolery: The finishing touch

The specific positioning of One's jewellery communicates clear messages much in the vein of semaphore or Morse code. For many suburban house-wives, the disposition of jewellery has become a contemporary equivalent to eighteenth-century fan language, allowing them to remain mute but say so very much to their husbands, lovers, friends and pool boys. The following are a few of the most basic communications observed during one month of dinner parties in Surrey.

Beware – my husband suspects	Phone for a Date!	Phone for the fish knives, Norman!	TAKE ME! TAKE ME! You huge great hairy chartered accountant, you
The coast is clear! What's left of my mother-in-law is in that bin liner over there	Please pass the gravy	Does anyone know any jokes?	I'm a sucker for an Earl, but for a Duke I'll swallow

When Even Your Tailor Can Do No More — D.I.Y. surgery:

It may be inevitable that tailoring, make-up, seamage, powdering, plumping and perming is not enough. It's at this point that One should reach for the tool kit under the stairs. Cosmetic surgery is expensive and all too often prone to going wrong, which is not the fault of the procedure but all too often the fault of the surgeon. Really, it's foolish to trust a stranger (some One who has only just met the face they are about to carve up) with the all too important responsibility of making One look better.

A large mirror with a well-lit view of the condemned features, coloured felt-tip pens, sharp implements and a stiff gin are really all One needs. The secret to success with auto-rhinoplasty is to choose your inspiration wisely and to be careful what you wish for.

Aesthetic surgery at home: A countdown

10) Never underestimate the effect a tightly ratcheted pony-tail has on eye-bags. But make the effect permanent with a few staples behind the ears.

9) Go classic: bee-stung lips (for that sultry pre-Raphaelite look) are easily achieved with actual bees.

8) Break as many veins as possible on One's cheeks for permanent blusher.

7) Pin sticky-out ears back with pins, better still – nails.

6) Professional liposuction is unnecessary when One bears in mind every home has a Hoover and every kitchen drawer a set of skewers.

5) Treating fat people with stomach-stapling is well known, but try stapling their stomach to their faces so there's nowhere to insert food.

4) Gender reassignment itself is not difficult but, unfortunately, there are at the moment only two genders from which to choose.

3) Bottom lifts are very popular. But be warned: lifts go down as well as up (and indeed sometimes get stuck between floors).

2) Breast augmentation – augment breasts with all sorts of unusual shiny decorative things.

1) Hair transplants without surgery – attach weights to One's genitalia. After a few years, the hairy parts in question will become pliable and stretchy enough to pull over One's head and be worn as a hirsute hood.

Happy Hacking!

CHAPTER THREE

One's
Communication

Communicating with Confidence

The $\mathcal{P}osh$, bless them, know only too well that no matter how exquisite a toilette or how symphonic an outfit, it won't last for ever. No, to make a really decent dent on $\mathcal{P}oshterity$, One needs to say (or better still, write down. Even better yet, *have written down* by some One good at writing) lovely things of $\mathcal{P}oshness$ and importance.

When Correct Form roamed the earth laying waste to independence and creativity, the way One communicated and what One communicated were tightly controlled. Having a class came with a particular way of speaking or, more accurately, it was presumed that the way One spoke signified the speaker's membership of a particular class. That, thanks to the almost free-form jazz attitude society has now evolved for itself, has been well and truly subverted. Nobs are just as likely to speak with the lazy splutter formerly associated with fruit and veg markets, whilst even taxi drivers may these days sound more than a little bit Fulham.

For those ordinary people who have the insight and self-knowledge to understand their lives really do need a Pinch of $\mathcal{P}osh$, our Authors (whose perfect enunciation could cut crystal) suggest the following.

First and foremost, say what needs saying, write what needs writing or txt wt nds txtng with commitment (and a lovely light-reflective smile). If One has any doubts whatsoever about what One is about to express – don't express it. If it is badly thought, shoddily punctuated, poorly polished or in any way mispronounced, then don't allow it out. Look lovely instead.

One's communication always used to be the yardstick by which One's social position was appraised. Communication communicated exactly which herd One belonged to. Theoretically, mutton could *dress* as lamb, and wolves could *assume* sheep's clothing, but the minute either opened their snouts, there'd be a compromising bleat or an inappropriate snarl.

Communication really depends quite simply on confidence. If confidently delivered, no One will doubt the value of what is being communicated – whereas any attempt to express an opinion or state a view without an appropriate emphatic polish will self-scupper the communication right from the very start. Watch it sink, watch it sink.

The Spoken Word: How One speaks says a lot about One. Rules are made to be spoken

For the upper classes, it was once that the simple act of talking (or indeed sending a postcard from some elegant seaside resort) required a choreographed butterfly ballet of stylised flourishes and sinuous sentence structures. All rather honeyed, all rather lovely, all specifically contrived to prove in what high esteem the conversationalists held each other. However, it meant that communications, quite so frothily whipped up in their own Viennese cream, were inconvenient if One had an urgent message, such as badly needing a drink, evacuating a burning pleasure dome, or evacuating a red-hot bowel.

So it does make sense (One supposes somewhat regretfully) that communication in our age should be more tailored, more severe, less inclined to hyperbole (every last bit of it). Life nowadays moves so fast, pleasure domes burn so very quickly, and the Internet launches our words around a new virtual world before One has a chance to spell(-check) it properly, so it seems we must now be firm and use one word where three perfectly lovely words would once have done so terribly, awfully, perfectly well.

Regional Accents:
The rin in spin stis minly on the plin

Without the benefit of television or pocket pagers, Neolithic communities devised numerous ways of using their gullets to make noises. These guttural noises (or accents as they are better known today) could vary radically from valley to valley. And, since every One spoke differently, there was no real perception of a correct or an incorrect way of saying ordinary things.

Even as recently as the black-toothed court of Elizabeth I, *über*-courtiers like Francis Drake were permitted to have Devonshire accents which today would be horribly discriminated against, since it would show too close a family connection with the village idiot. But then, Sir Francis was rather special, what with his charming, pointy little beard and a standing room only codpiece.

No, it was later, more geographically sensitive ages, which decided that one bit of the country was 'better' than another and therefore suggested that speaking as Southerners speak was miles better than oinking like Northerners oink.

Speaking proper
Over the years, an extraordinary way of speaking was woven out of numerous influences and dialects to create what became perceived as correct speech. Since it's more of a speech impediment than an accent, it can be aped by attaching painful bulldog clips to One's upper lip. This causes One's consonants to be clipped as tight as a topiary hedge and renders all irritable vowels an impossibility. It is what happens when One tries to communicate with a stiff upper lip.

The antithesis, communication at its most incorrect, is speech in which vowels are not only stressed but augmented, joined by other over-friendly vowels or softer consonants, to create spoken words of rich juiciness. Words that reverberate with fleshy, tripelike judderings.

Thus:

Word	Correct Pronunciation	Incorrect Pronunciation
Flower	Flar	Floowarr
House	Hise	Aoorwse
Isn't	Int	Aintt-ah
Mouth	Moith	Maarff-ah
Yes	Eas	Yayrrs

Regional accents are now very, very much in vogue, because people of a politically correct persuasion want every One to feel loved. They want to love the most the Ones who speak the funniest (like Cockernys or the Scottish), so they give them jobs in government. One should understand that regional accents came about as the people in the regions battled with pluck, spunk and vigour to overcome the extreme weather conditions that occur in places ending in 'Thorp' or 'Thistle'. There, high winds or odd acoustics caused by extraordinary rock formations inspired local humans over time to develop specific ways of talking using deposits of mucus stored at the back of their throats. In the middle of Britainfordshire, where people have been burning things for pleasure or profit since the Iron Age, they speak through slits at the back of their soft palates and only chat in the most lugubrious of ways. In the west of the country, where every One eats thick rich cream all the time, they speak creamily. Whilst in the east, they're taught to speak like wind-blown gates hung on rusty hinges.

Regional accents are quite, quite fascinating, and starting a collection is both rewarding and diverting. Regional accents may be collected in well-washed-out jam jars through a large funnel similar to those on wind-up gramophones. Do ensure they're labelled correctly.

Foreign Accents: The pain of Spain

Foreign people, who were not brought up speaking British in nurseries, now regret it. British has become the Lingua Franca *de nos jours*. (Or Frank's tongue of our times, by way of translation.)

Everything important, like road signs and the washing instructions in expensive knitwear, is printed in British, which means that every One everywhere needs to understand British words. Cleverly, all popular music and most films come in British so that foreign people may practise whilst watching television or relaxing. This is to be expected really, since British is a nice clear language which even dogs understand.

The way that British is spoken can give One an extremely good idea of where a person comes from, which enables One to kick off a conversation with a specific comment about their point of origin, such as, 'Ahah, I say, good man, I guess from the way you roll your "R"s you simply must be from San Francisco.' So, as an aid, study the following question as spoken by a variety of denizens of the planet in order that One may recognise their ways of speaking.

Hello, how do you do? Where may I hang my hat please?
– A British person
Allo, oi di yi dee? Hwere me I 'ang mi yat pliz?
– A French person

Hillo, hi du yow du? Whirr may I hung me 'at plouse?
– A Scottish person

Harro, ow dee yay di? Qwera mai hi 'eng ma hat plarse?
– A Dutchish person

Eeeee, hooo do yooo dooo? Wooo moo hoo oong moo hoot plooo?
– A person eating a most hot potato

Eeeee, hooe doe yoe doe? Wooo m'ooo ong me hoot plose?
– An oriental person eating a most hot potato

Hiya, cowboy, 'ow de do? Where may I hang me hat sirree?
– A person from America

Heeeeee dede? Weee meee hangee hatee plee?
– A most inebriated person from New Zealandshire

11000111111101100001101 111111001010101010000111111?
– A binary person

Hee dee do? Whereth may I hangeth me hath, plithee?
– An Anglo-Saxon person (although there aren't many around)

The telephone voice: an ancient British art form

There are times, British people believe, when it is extraordinarily important to sound like Mary Poppins with a mouthful of frozen peas. It's a mystery why. It's not as simple as setting out just to sound upper class, since half the appeal seems to be in sounding very, very old-fashioned. It's referred to as a 'telephone voice', and all British people have one somewhere. Since telephones were first invented, people felt they had to sound much better than they actually did in case a reigning monarch rang them accidentally.

The 'Home-Made-Gent', it was thought, could pay for grace at the right tailor but would be unable ever to order a light supper at the Savoy Grill without exposing his state-educated roots to chilly ridicule. What sport there was to be had watching, from a safe distance, the telephone voice falter and crackle under the gimlet stare of a seriously swanky *maître d'* as it limped and hobbled over the rocks and hurdles of menu French.

People now use telephone voices to complain in restaurants, engage household staff and enquire the price of things in the gift shops of large stately homes open to the public (presumably in the vain hope that others will think they live there).

Cockernys and Mockernys

For other times, such as when One wishes to sound as if One is one of the gang (One presumes the 'gang' being of footpads of cut-purses), One speaks Mockerny. It's the opposite of a telephone voice and requires the ending sound of every word to be unpronounced. There was recently a tremendous vogue to mockernyate, and everywhere every One went, perfectly nicely brought-up people spoke as if with a club tongue, using a vocabulary of barely five and twenty words.

Needless to say, this dark and pointless period in our recent history led to a dramatic fall in the birth rate, since no One in their right mind wanted to do sex or mate with some One that spoke Mockerny.

Cockernys are like Mockernys, the difference being, they're not actually faking it. They also have their own Cockerny vocabulary based on rhyming couplets. Some people think Shakespeare may have had a hand in it, but it was more likely to have been Christopher Marlowe (who wrote all the best bits of Shakespeare in his spare time).

Since Cockerny Couplets (or Cockerny rhyming slang, as Cockernys themselves refer to it) are so very amusing, our ever indulgent Authors explain below some useful phrases and their *Posh* translations.

Cockerny Couplets	British English	Poshish English
Apples and pears	Stairs	The sweeping swoosh from one floor to another
Barnet Fair	Hair	Coiffeur
Garlic stench	French	Cheese-eating surrender monkey
He's a bit play for today	He's gay	Have you met my *Poshterior* decorator?
J. Arthur Rank	Wank	Self-pollution, Oneanism
Raspberry Ripple	Nipple	Pert pink pearl of paradise
Sherbert Dab	Cab	A share-a-chauffeur
Tom-Dick	Sick	Oyster poisoning
Thruppeny bits	Tits (or other small migratory birds)	Pert pink pearls of paradise
Trouble and strife	Wife	Darling
Whistle and flute	Suit	The very least One should have on

The Words One Speaks

Being interesting really ought to be compulsory. It's a shame it isn't, really. Truly Posh people are always interesting and say interesting things in interesting, glamorous ways. What One says when One speaks is obviously enormously important: it should be elegant, sophisticated and so exquisitely civilised that birds stop singing in the trees just so they may hear the conversation better. Making sense, however, is only rarely compulsory, but it is nice if One can.

Anyone with enough leisure time to think up new and amusing ways of saying 'arse' is worth getting to know.

Posh vocabulary

It really is a terribly good idea to have an enormous vocabulary of useful lovely words which One can string together into jewel-like ornaments. Here are some marvellous words with which to decorate One's mouth:

A

Abysmal – deeply bad, like a deep, deep, deep cleft of badness

Akimbo – a useful technique for doing sex

Amphibious – having an ability to both surf and turf in between the sheets

Awfully – very

B

Bloccoco – a gentleman in a powdered wig with whom One wouldn't want to mess

Bushmaster – a lady whisperer, a gentleman adept at lady-wrangling

Butleriferous – to do something around the house rather nicely

C

Chaiselongulous – a middle-aged floppishness in ladies

Charmoury – the methods of charm at One's disposal

Commedia dell'arte – eighteenth-century Venetian television

D

Daisy chain – a line of alternating ladies and gentlemen, all within each other's person

Décolletage – the ornamental front of a lady shown to all at official do's

Deflagrate – One's duty if wind has broken in a confined space

E

Eminence – a hillock or some One further up the food chain than One

Engorgeous – to make marvellously longer, thicker and more full of throbbing

Entropy – the inevitability of disorder. Nature at its very worst and indeed most Venetian

F

Fresian – chic monochrome cattle

Fubsy – fully rounded

Full-fat – highly decorative interior decoration

Full-frontal – the nicest thing married people may show each other

G

Genticity – the contemporary form of gentility (i.e. being nice but without a compulsory use of lace)

Gorblimey – a marvellous expletive for moments of enthusiasm

Grumpertary – a body or society of bad-tempered people prone to belittlement of others

H

Haunch – the bit that fills the top part of a gentleman's trousers

Homosexualist – Ancient Greek gentlemen who loved their own sort

Homosexualistic – to do something well but fussily

Hotten totenous – to have something over stuffed and bottomy

I

In flagrante delicto – caught with One's hand in the till (sexually speaking)

Insufflate – to blow One's friend up through their nose

Intumescent – something so lovely and so very plumpy when swollen with pleasure

Irenically – to do something to encourage peace

J

Jabot – an ornamental frill of the foreskin

Jade – a slut or hussy, harlot or minor celebrity, in general

Jousting – an old-fashioned but fun event for the Sportistic

Justifiable homicide – an end to be looked forward to by street eaters, under-groomers and estate mongers

K

King Charles Spaniel – dog of dogs

Kinky – a little bit more relaxed in the bed chamber than most

Kiosk – a Turkish gazebo

Krillions – a lot, lot, lot of very small things

Krugerrand – the best currency with which to buy somewhere to live

Kyliscious – boomerang-like or Kylie-like

L

Laurentian – as done by a Laurence

Levée – getting dressed in public first thing in the morning

Licentious – so lovely it hurts again and again and again

Lickety-spit – a very, very quick way of doing sex

Lothario – One who loves and leaves and sells their story to the tabloids

M

Millinery – the dark arts of hat-making

Milord – a term still used by foreign people for a Posh gentleman visiting their lovely shores

Mockerny – a disastrous way of speaking

Mumbo-bimbo – new age practices believed in only by ladies

Myriad – lots of myrs

N

Negaraea – the black art of seeing everything blackly

Noblesse oblige – The responsibility of the Posh

Novocaine – almost as much fun as gin and tonic

Nubility – the way One feels about One's recently post-pubescent relations

Nymphaeum – where Nymphs live

O

Oboe d'amore – bizarrely not a euphemism but a real instrument

Oboe (pink) – a euphemism

Ogee – one of the more elegant arches

Overblown – going a little too far with a neckscarf

Oversleeve – a sleeve worn over another sleeve, quite uncannily

P

Peasantry – a jolly lot, rather carbohydratey, who no longer really exist

Persiflage – waffle

Puissance – to have great power and large dimensions

Pursuance – to carry out or to carry on with something despite every One else laughing

Q

Quakerish – rather plain and unfussy. Oatmeally

Quinine – what makes gin and tonic what it is

Quintessence – the most essential bit of anything, the thickest, most gloopy, most flavourful part

Quornish – to be grey and flaccid

R

Recussant – One who deliberately breaks all the rules of nice behaviour

Red Leicestershireish – to be cheesy and orange

Rigmarole – a complicated procedure requiring lots of application i.e. getting dressed

Rockery – a garden feature best avoided

S

Sinisteral – interestingly left-handed

Spam – tinned meat which doesn't require One to have teeth to eat

Strigil – what the Romans used in the bath

Swizzlestick – one of the true badges of civilisation

Syrup stirrup (Cockerny slang) – the chin strap of a wig

T

Thong – minimalist under-things

Tiarish – something quite out of date but still rather stylish

Tonic water – the drink of the Gods

Triumphal arch – a nice thing to ornament One's front garden

U

Ulterior – the background of an interior

Unicorn – a delicious animal rather like zebra in texture, best served with a New World rosé

Utensil – a horrid word

Utility – another horrid word

Uxorious – to be fond of One's wife

V

Valhalla – where hyper-borean people go once they've been run over by a tractor

Van Dyck – Dutch ladies who no longer eat meat

Velutinous – covered in ravishingly soft fine hairs like a peach or an anorexic

Vintage – an object or frock of dubious aesthetics sold for an unfeasible amount of money

W

Waspie – a marvellous device of intimate female apparel to create a tiny waist

Whatnot – a lovely piece of furniture for displaying collections of whatevers

Wisp – literally, a small handful of straw

Wunderkind – a German child who writes passable poems

XYZ

Xanthic – yellow and not in a good way

Xu – money used by Vietnamese people

Yachtish – an aquatic experience with pretensions

Zeitgeist – an intellectualish term for vogue

Zoomorphic – looking like or turning into animals

Zouave – large French Gorblimey trousers

It is our astonishingly well-presented Authors' opinion, gleaned from many, many decades of speaking, that inelegant language can do mortal damage to a society's self-esteem and should be avoided at any cost. Far worse, inelegant language using inelegant words can lead, if unchecked, to a society which eventually turns its back on tailoring.

Correct Form created for itself vexatious minefields of conversational prejudice to sort the wheat from the chav. As a result, unfortunately and most regrettably, speaking nicely gained something of a bad reputation, with the presupposition that any elegant locutor or locutrix was really just a very nasty old snob. Bollocks really. So it's the duty of all, when One thinks about it, to assimilate elegance in speech and make it available for all.

And so, with elegance the quarry and eloquence the prize, please address the following:

Overt-familiarity

Using words regularly (sometimes three or four times a day) doesn't mean that One should shorten them for ease. Sawing the end off one word, or hatcheting the beginning of the next shows locutional laziness. There are some who do this very much on purpose just to give the impression that it's a word they use so often, they simply cannot be bothered to expend the effort to shape the whole word on their mean and thin lips. It shows a person who grudges the effort to speak to another. Not friendly, really.

The word 'phone' is a good example. One must suppose that 'phone' (a very ugly word, by the way) is 'telephone' shortened. Although, of course, it could be gramophone, francophone, headphone, xylophone or ET phone-home. It's all very unclear. And as for any One using the term 'Yorkshire', presumably as a shortening for 'Yorkshire Pudding', then they really should remember there was also a 'Yorkshire Ripper' as well.

'Bike' (as in 'bicycle') is another ugly shortening, although 'cycle' as in menstrual isn't really any better. It's best really in this specific case to refer to the object in question betwixt your thighs as a 'chopper'. If in doubt, fall back on a trade name.

'Van' as a shortening for 'caravan' takes an unbelievably unattractive idea and makes it shorter and more stunted. And, as if that weren't bad enough, there's the overly familiar term 'telly' used by those who do nothing other than achieve prolonged intimacy with their television. One can recognise them by their close-set mole-like eyes, the generously flesh-swagged swollen torsos and malodorous golden circle on the front of their Sportistic trousers.

Snob Speak

There's a higher level of horror to overt-familiarity: Snob Speak. This is when words, or more often the names of upmarket, shiny shops, are shortened in an attention-grabbing, self-conscious way. People who speak loudly about hampers from 'Fortnums' or the fact that Terry took them out for a spin in the 'Rolls' will, One hopes, suffer a terrifyingly painful afterlife.

The euphemism: A kindness or a curse?

Once upon a time, euphemisms were looked down upon as conversational devices employed tactfully to shroud and occlude a frightful concept or bestial word by means of a linguistic smokescreen. However, euphemisms should be well and truly applauded as one of the better ideas for the British language (apart from the fact that they're Greek).

The secret of top-level Olympic Gold-winning euphemism is never to copy any One else's euphemisms and also never ever to use the same euphemism twice. No, see the creation of heavily swagged euphemisms engorgeoused with gilded cherubs and enormous tassels as an exciting creative outlet. For One's own amusement, dream up euphemisms for everyday objects, like One's own lovely genitals perhaps, or the almost as lovely genitals of a friend. No, a decent euphemism is like an everyday sonnet which can take a common or garden predicament like 'glans rash', 'pubic razor burn', 'habitual halitosis' or 'occasional kleptomania' and turn it into something so very much more romantic-sounding. If nothing else, the generous use of original euphemism in conversation is evidence of someone with enough leisure time to think up new and more decorative ways of saying 'arse'.

The silent words of British-speak

In the noble and densely lovely British language, there are various traditions and customs which are really not worth tinkering with. They exist to confuse people of foreignness – most particularly, the French – so they're worth learning by heart. All of them involve a silent word which remains unpronounced and are legalised examples of overt-familiarity in that they show a familiarity of the subject by means of what One doesn't say.

For example, the art of racing horses is never horse-racing. Thanks to an act of generosity from the loveliest of monarchs, Charles II, 'horse' is silent and forever implied by the term 'racing'. And so, any other racing, be it camel, dog, greyhound, badger or lesbian, has to be specified.

Other terms that are subject to this rule are:

STATION – 'Train' is always implied, which means that 'bus', 'work', 'polling', 'police' and 'ideas above One's' all require at least another word to justify their existence.

RIDING – 'Horse', just as with 'racing' is implied and therefore silent. In fact, anyone using the term 'horse riding' should be forcefully admonished with a flexible bamboo switch or a less flexible house brick.

BAG – 'Hand', as in handbag, has through evolution been omitted, leaving the way open for body, rat, scum, overnight, and fag.

Foreign words and what they're for

The fact that people of the world use completely different words and ways to speak is deeply inconvenient. Or at least it would be if no One understood speaking British. The only race on earth who categorically refuse to speak, understand or acknowledge speaking British are the French. They are very, very bitter that French is no longer the international language of culture – which, up until a hundred years ago, it was. The French are also bitter that the British won the Battle of Waterloo, and they'll often moan at the British about how they tragically lost family at Waterloo. If this happens to you, ask them which platform. This will make them very cross.

In retaliation, the British have made up a variety of French expressions the French themselves refuse to accept as French. Here are a few:

A FOU RIRE – to laugh when One really mustn't, such as at the French

APRÈS NOUS LE DÉLUGE – to get so drunk One unconsciously unleashes enough liquid to float an ark

BOURGEOIS – cosy suburban Frenchdom, all lovely, rich sauces to cover up horse meat. Or rat

CHAISE LONGUE – the term that inspired the heinous word 'lounge'

CONSOMMÉ – very, very thin soup. Possibly made from something which, but a few minutes before, was slithering up the garden path

EPATER LES BOURGEOIS – to slap the cosy French suburbs round the rosy cheeks with a pair of pig-skin gloves

LAISSEZ LES BON TEMPS ROULER – to get drunk

LANGUE DU CHAT – a biscuit inspired by the shape and abrasive texture of a hastily removed cat's tongue. Rather revolting really

SALON – where One gets One's hair dyed lilac

SANG FROID – stiff upper lip

SOIRÉE – an evening get-together with no food but a lot of pretension

In complete contrast to the French, the Italians are gregarious and accepting. Since so much of all Western language derives from the tongue of their Latin forebears, One can see why their generosity comes easily. With the rather affected exception of '*ciao*' aside, the influence of Italian is constrained linguistically to 'linguine', 'pizza', 'espresso', 'bruschetta' and 'macchiato'. For so jolly and social a race, it's no surprise the real debt One owes the lovely, if hirsute, Italians is culinary. But other Italian words are also useful:

BELLA – beautiful, but in British translated as, 'Dowdy clothes shop for Home Counties ladies of amplitude'

CAMERA – which bizarrely means 'room', not 'camera' at all

PREGO – which means virtually nothing but gets said a lot

QUATTROCENTO – which means 'fourteenth-century', unlike in British, where 'fourteenth century' actually means a century in which all the years begin with thirteen

UOMO – means 'homo' or at least looking like, particularly in the context of Gentleman's swimming things

USCITA – a really marvellous way of saying exit

Germanistic words are rarely used. They're often just right for moments of considerable Gothicism, so anyone dropping *schadenfreude*, *stürm und drang* or '*götterdämmerung*' into a conversation is probably a deeply self-conscious undergraduate or an out-of-work restaurant critic.

Smorgasbord is the only word to have come into mainstream speak from Scandinavia. In Scandinavian, it means 'smorgasbord'.

America tends not specifically to invent new words for the old world (although both political-over-compensation speak and businessspeak come from there). But it does take old world words and make them new and shiny for their own purposes, for example, 'gifting' (giving presents), 'makeover' (paper over the cracks), 'differently abled' (pluckily unable), 'timepoor' (busy), 'friendly fire' (unfriendly fire), 'awesome" (not bad). American people love words to sound much, much louder than they actually are.

Swearing: A blessing or a ****ing curse?

There really is nothing more glamorous or more sophisticated than an exquisitely modulated whiplash of expletives drawled with an elegant offhandedness. But, as with euphemisms, which require a similar art, use as many *original* swear words as possible. Most importantly, swear without shame or self-consciousness. Far from being a rudeness when someone swears energetically, it demonstrates that they feel an unpatronising sense of comradeship with One. A few casual 'F' words must be seen as a token of friendship, an emphatic gesture which illustrates One's relationship has gone beyond superficial, unproductive Correct Form.

Here are some super swear words and fantastically frightful insults:

Verb	Object	Cuntext
eniferating	miss-moss	A skadiloping pinch piss
exfulcherating	ladylard	A munting knupple
gong-ferming	flep	A vaginating pip licker
munting	cankymillander	How far to the Cotswolds?
postulating	mank	A wastering clyte-fist
seeping	cleft wax	A self-bothering speight
self-polluting	plushnuts	Flep off, fulch monkey
silting	smunt	A fremulinous glist
suppurating	lickwad	A fulching flap mechanic
vaginating	ansyboshtups	A complete cannute
wasttering	huffmunck	Pustulating miss-moss
whoring	fissure fluff	An exfulcherating mink-muncher

So, now that form and function have been so deliciously drawn together the time has now come to explore One's conversation. The delicate balance of how and what One says will forever be the very pinnacle of civilisation.

Conversation starters One should have at One's disposal at all times

* 'The weather's looking up' (a conversation of such beigeness all will feel able to join in)
* 'Your garden is *ravishing*, please do tell what your secret is?' (a universal conversation for garden parties and orgies)
* 'I say, those warts on the side of your neck appear to have become snagged in your necklace. Do let me help. You know, it reminds me of a funny story . . .' (perfect opening gambit for the British Royal family)
* 'I have to say, I think Oscar Wilde was really rather misunderstood. You know he did girls, too . . .' (a great way of breaking the ice at seminaries)
* 'I had a friend at school who kept silkworms in her sports knickers. Well, one morning when the radiators got stuck on 'high', they hatched and . . .' (a marvellous opening gambit for manic depressives. They'll laugh until they cry, literally)
* 'Phwoarr' (marvelous for a room full of builderators, although One must demonstrate that the phwoarr is not directed at any of them)
* 'My favourite beast of burden is the ass. What's yours?' (a great conversation to have anywhere in the world)
* 'Now, what would you like to know about me?' (without a shadow of doubt, the very, very best way of starting any conversation)

These are all very well for situations in which there is no immediate expectation of physical danger. Our concerned and wonderfully hand-washed

Authors more than understand that the conversations One really needs to have ready in One's pocket at all times are those suitable for life-threatening situations such as being marooned without One's driver in the middle of a social housing project, being stuck in a lift, in a submarine, or indeed, stuck in a Duchess.

The secret is to talk slowly with a soothing modulated tone and not to hold back on the sparkle. Start simply, 'You know this reminds me of ...', and then start painting a conversational picture of such compelling detail, the situation at hand is quite occluded: '... the time a friend of a friend had a little too much to drink and felt inspired to show us all quite how far foreskins stretch under the right conditions.' Time will pass most quickly indeed.

Titles: A beginners' guide

In Britain, there is the British way, which, when compared with all other ways, is the best, despite its numerous flaws. The British way (perhaps derived from some ancient Druidic ritual or other) requires three people at all times: one to do the introducing, one to be introduced and one to receive the introduction. It allows British people not to have to say their own name, about which they may feel embarrassed or modest.

The modesty bit is important whether One's title is Mrs, Mr, Count, Duchess, Laird, Wing-Commander, Postmaster or any of the other options considered suitable to receive the better sort of junk mail, but One must not use it in conversation about One's self. But, this is where the British way gets complicated. Even though, in a One-to-One context, One says, 'Hi, I'm Andrew, Uldmilla, Hermasita or, indeed, Jove,' One's actually deep down hoping the introducee is nevertheless going to respond, 'How do you do your ...' (Grace, Ladyship, Constable or God of my fathers).

Our Authors, in their gilded cloud of glory, know many, many people of title. And the sort of people of title our lovely Authors know prefer to be addressed with their proper title simply so they may most kindly insist on not being addressed with their proper title as a way of showing intimacy, friendship and respect for their addressee. But, be warned, not all people of title are as lovely as those who boast intimacy with our magnetic Authors. So, to help, here's a quick rundown of the most popular people of titles and how One should address them:

KING/QUEEN – Your Majesty, then Sir or Ma'am (pronounced 'mam', as in 'jam')

HRH, A PRINCE – Your Royal Highness, then Sir (if an introduction to be called 'Chaz' is not forthcoming from the Sir in question)

HRH, A PRINCESS – Your Royal Highness, then darling

A CELEBRATED COURTESAN – Madame

A PRESIDENT – Mr President, Sir

A MILKMAN – Milkie

AN ARCHBISHOP – Your Grace

A DUKE – Your Grace

A DUCHESS – Your Gracie

A CARDINAL – Your Eminence

MRS LLEWELYN-BOWEN – Madam

MR LLEWELYN-BOWEN – Bloke

A PUNTER – My Pleasure

A COUNTESS – My Lady

A BISHOP – My Lord

A RABBI – Your Lord

A MARQUESS – Lord

A BISHOP *in flagrante delicto* – Good Lord

ELVIS – Your Majesty

A COURTESAN PAST HER PRIME – Your Vagesty

A DUKE DRESSED AS A COURTESAN PAST HER PRIME – Your Travesty (see picture)

And for those without titles, God invented names

Don't feel bad. If every single One of us were titled, then titles really wouldn't be special, would they? In fact, thinking about it, having a name is every bit as good as having a title and should be treated in more or less the same way.

Remember: as with titles, assume the formal and wait (One hopes not too long) for an invitation to use the informal form of address. If a wife refers to her husband in your presence by his given name (some husbands do indeed have given names), then it should be treated as an invitation for One to do the same. If, however, she refers to him as Mr Knobchuck, then Mr Knobchuck should he be to you.

The Written Word: The last bastion of Correct Form

There is an explicit formality in 'putting something in writing', which means that One really does have to know One's way around the desiccated, cobwebby old maze of etiquette. This is probably why so many people today avoid writing and prefer txting or mail-Eing.

Writing a Posh Letter Poshly

Writing a Posh letter Poshly (or, indeed, a list, poem, thank-you letter, French letter, libel letter, invoice or an advertisement to be placed in a Newsagents' window offering One's services of correction) should be enjoyed wholeheartedly. One so rarely treats One's self to the opportunity to see the exquisite squiggles and elegant swirls of One's handwriting emerge, cavort and playfully consort across the surface of really very good-quality writing paper.

Take lascivious delight in choosing an unusual shade of ink, encourage the most sensual feelings within One's inner being at the living touch of parchment or, better still, vellum and play games of playful pain with the venal, inescapable heat of molten sealing wax. It really is rather surprising that people don't write *Posh* letters *Poshly* more often.

Psh txtng

A sad and rather lonely man was sacked from his job. (It made him very bitter indeed to be out of work and out of money.) For many, many years, he had made quite a good living advertising houses for sale by translating ordinary sentences into meaningless jumbles of vowel-less words. It was he who coined the term 'bedsit' (from, One supposes, 'bed sitting room') and 'mod cons' (from 'modern conveniences'). But now the hateful fellow was destitute and, in his vileness, he sought revenge. And his revenge was mighty, for his revenge was the contemporary scourge that is … text speak (or rather, txt spk).

So now, rather than using One's thumbs to polish off a message properly, with the required consonants, vowels and punctuation, One instead receives communications such as 'sorE 4 bng L8 will CU L8r. Luv'.

Txt spks, ugly + crp. Txt spkrs all hv hllitosis + flln archs + no frnds. In fct thr all fckn cnts.

And So, Whither our Wonderful Language? A Somewhat Melancholy Indulgence of a Postscript

How well do we communicate today? Language, like so much of society around us, seems set on a vigorous course of regression. Words have become shorter, sentences a patchwork of syntax, and conversations mindless repetitive backfill e.g., 'you know what I mean, I hear what you're saying, um actually um awesome at the end of the day,' etc., etc., etc. And as for the written word? Well, it's no longer written but generated from a digitised palette of binary possibilities.

There are no excuses for inelegance, ever. And, yes, it may take much longer to tap out without One's predictive txt facility that, 'luncheon at twelve thirty would be simply lovely,' but, then, that's so very much the point of Posh. It's all about effort over ease, consideration rather than condescension.

So, what's left? What is the only unsullied method of communication left to the Posh? Graffiti, that's what. Brothers, sisters, let's get tagging! Choose a car spray of your favourite hue, dangle over a railway bridge and spray till One may spray no more:

the WONDERFULNESS OF WONDERFUL ONE

CHAPTER FOUR

One's Situation

Understanding One's Situation in Three Easy Steps

Step 1: One's Financial Situation

Formerly, when One defined One's financial situation (i.e., job, lack of job or refusal even to entertain the idea of a job), One defined One's class and, ultimately, One. At the top of the employment tree, there was not having a job at all; and at the bottom, there was working very hard at a job whose only perk was access to an all-you-can eat cesspit (and some truly unusual scabs). But, quite honestly, how One's day is filled or from which stagnant gene pool One's great-grandparents emerged couldn't be less relevant, because to be truly Posh is not to be defined by One's situation but by One's acts as a humanoid – which is a relief, for it means that One can get on with Onedom and with the task of creating and enjoying loveliness. There is, after all, nothing more boring than talking about jobs or family when One could be talking about One, which is always quite captivating. Although, having said that, there are things that One can get up to with soft fluffy underpants and leather straps that never cease to fascinate.

Never forget that 'marvellous manners' always was an exclusive system designed to keep anyone not from the upper classes in their place. Over the years, a patois developed which allowed the prejudiced to judge any One's social position based on a handful of set criteria. And One's situation gave away too much class ammunition. One was socially scent-marked by it. And should One be unhappy with the particular *odeur de* class One was born with, One had to lie or pretend to have violent choking fits whenever One's 'situation' was enquired after. But, now that even plumbers are *Posh*, now that any One can move to the Cotswolds and now that HM the Queen of England's predilection for storing Cornflakes in Tupperware has been revealed, One's situation really is up to One and One alone.

As something of an exemplar of how so much has changed, please digest the following chart:

Old situation	*New* situation
Plutonically wealthy Duke of one of the larger northern counties	Soap Star
Fabulously titled heiress with cash literally to burn and diamonds the size of hubcaps	Glamour Model turned Soap Star
Rat-Catcher	Television Celebrity
Rat-Catcher's Assistant	Stockbroker
Gentleman Farmer	Animal Rights Activist
Leper	Footballer

Old situation	New situation
Leperess	Footballer's Wife
Quite the loveliest courtesan at court	Airline Stewardess
Gentleman's Gentleman	Gentleman's Gentleman with an after-hours position in the seedier sort of youth hostel
Lady's Maid	Umbrella Model
Reigning Monarch of a medium-sized, land-locked European country	Manager of a medium-sized three-star hotel
Stable boy	Gentleman's Undergarment Model
Court Jester	Manic Depressive
Curate	Computer Programmer
Rector	Erector
Knight-at Arms	Security Guard
Shit-Shoveller	Tabloid Journalist
Swineherd	Tabloid Editor
Page	Haemorrhoid Model
Squire with a decent enough living, a few hundred acres in Wiltshire and an elegantly symmetrical Georgian mansion	Geisha Boy

Can Money Ever be Posh?

The pursuit of money is, very obviously, never ever going to be Posh. Technically speaking, Posh lives are best and most efficiently lived in a money-less vacuum. Ironically, this can only really be achieved by the acquisition of enormous mounds of cash. The brutal, chilly truth is that money really is required in order that it may be exchanged for shiny things. But, far worse than that, money has to be earned. In fact, One really has to commit an enormous amount of One's day to the buying of sparkling things just to ensure that the levels of cash in One's account never rise beyond a certain point. It can be exhausting, which is a fact that is so often overlooked (deliberately) by the rest of the world. And, besides, without the Posh, where would the global sparkling-things market be? Why, there'd be gluts of seventeenth-century tapestries and mountains of Casa Blanca lilies mouldering pointlessly, and a planet much less civilised. In the absence of money, the poor Posh soul is forced to face the world outside and actually find a job.

Can Jobs Ever be Posh?

When civilisation dawned and every One started walking upright, life became a lot more complicated to organise. The previous system – treating nature as a perpetual double-ended buffet – was straightforward, but lacked polish. Dividing the tribe up into sub-groups in charge of basic chores required the instant evolution of a barter-like system, which, of course, eventually grew into the economy we all know and fail to understand today.

There is, One has to admit, a seductive simplicity in turning back the clock to become responsible for all One's own needs without the intervention of third parties such as tradesmen, fishmongers, wine merchants or even professionals such as doctors, mobile librarians or astral nutritionists. But the simple simplicity of a good life in the land of plenty is nothing but a romance.

Procuring a situation: The first steps — situations (prettily) vacant

The first step is to pick a job. Do go for something that requires a high level of polish and/or charm. Selling perfectly made, exquisitely packaged Posh things is really quite rewarding and, now that everything's done with credit cards, One doesn't need to touch actual money. Another possibility is looking after some One much richer but much less lovely than One's self.

Being dressed in gorgeous things is always popular, although models these days are often required to be the most extraordinary shapes and, since many of the Posh are indeed lovely but not 'classically beautiful', modelling is more difficult than it used to be. Besides, a lot of models are very, very ugly inside.

More vigorous situations, such as being a member of a lifeboat crew or an emergency cat-stuck-in-a-tree rescuer are glamorous, rewarding and intensely helpful, but since they're voluntary and money doesn't change hands, ultimately useless if it's money One is after. If money isn't what One is after, then this is professional heaven. The one downside is that high-vis clothing is ugly and, more importantly, impossible to accessorise.

The best solution is to invent One's own job. The thing to do really is to see whether there's something that no One can do as well as you and then charge people money when you do it to or for them. In fact, since Ones are so good at doing sex, charging for it is really not complicated. After all, it's all about sharing.

Invent One's own situation

Mixing business with pleasure: Doing sex with clients

Of course, if One's business is pleasure (which is Posh) or One's only pleasure is business (which is un-Posh), then it's essential to hang on to all dry-cleaning receipts in case they're tax deductible.

Having a job but not doing any work

Having a job but fundamentally not doing anything to earn One's salary couldn't be more *Posh*. Ideal situations to procure one:

* Chairman of a pointlessly large company
* Advertising executive
* Government advisor
* Masochist's whipping boy (masochists are reliable in that they'll always insist on being whipped themselves, leaving the young lad paid to be whipped rather at a loose end)
* President of somewhere (don't be a monarch – they never *stop* working)
* Personal banker
* Magician's assistant
* Ventriloquist's dummy
* Shop dummy
* Socialite
* Trepanner's drill-sharpener
* Clock-winder's supervisor
* Television presenter
* Celebrity

Bosses: They're not that complicated

The first thing One notices about bosses is that they are the boss of One. The next thing One notices about bosses is that they pay One. Bosses tend to be little people with rather fragile egos which need constant stroking, although *Posh* bosses aren't unheard of. The best way of approaching bosses is with low, soothing clicking noises, open hand signals and a degree of caution. By and large, as long as One is nice to them and lets them win at competitive sports, then bosses continue to give One money.

When good jobs go bad

Being fired means your boss won't be paying you any more and will be wanting you to go away quite soon, if not immediately. One may find other words attached to the statement 'You're fired,' such as 'smug bastard', 'useless bitch', 'the stain will never come out', and 'the company's lawyers will be in touch'.

If you have no boss to fire you, then the bank (where money is kept) will come and close your business down, taking anything of value to pay for all the things that were bought but never paid for. Bankruptcy, as this is known, is less harrowing than it sounds, since things of value – computers, photocopiers, telephone switchboards – are rarely lovely to look at and are deeply unmissable once they have been repossessed.

When good bankruptcy goes bad: Life in prison

Custodial sentences should really be seen as a perfectly splendid opportunity to get on with things without all the distractions of the outside world. In fact, prisons really aren't to be feared. In truth, they're nothing like as scary as motorway service stations or fast-food drive-thrus. Indeed, prisons are often chock-a-(cell)block with other Ones who've committed the odd indiscretion against the tax authorities.

A *Posh* inmate, as in every other situation in so gilded a life, will be raised and celebrated by all those lovely new chums made inside. A *Posh* inmate will quickly find a series of important roles in the enclosed community, such as writing letters for other inmates to send to loved Ones; sorting out disputes brought on by overlong exposure to *Who Wants to be a Millionaire*; and modelling for allegorical compositions constructed in spent matches.

Downsides of prison life include the food, which is a bit of a trial; living life solely in denim, which is irritating (both mentally and physically); the fact that floral arrangements are frowned upon; and the insufferable hell of overhead lighting. And, above all else, being vigilant to always, always, always stay on the *right* side of the sex bullies.

Celebrate your cell: Mini-makeovers in minutes

* Weave brightly coloured strips of acrylic between the window bars to make an exciting and contemporary 'stained-glass' lattice
* Re-grout! Opt for a new soft pastel coordinating grout for that soothing 'outside, inside' feel
* Work with what One's got – accentuate the chic monochrome of mattress ticking by shoving your bedclothes under the mattress
* Create a feature wall using a repeating pattern of topless women or bottomless men cut from magazines. A high gloss finish for that *über-cool* lacquer look may be achieved over time by constant burnishing
* Take a leaf out of the Shaker style book: hang chairs from the wall and make a rag rug from leftover processed-cheese wrappers

Being the Boss: Keeping and caring for household staff

If One finds One's self in the position of doing the employing, remember that household staff should be seen as professionals who work very hard to make One's life run smoothly. It can be a difficult position for all concerned, since it requires an inordinate amount of time in each other's company. With this in mind, it's often very successful if One employs a friend as household staff or, indeed, becomes friendly with the household staff. Your beloved Authors keep numerous household staff, and all say they are extremely happy and fulfilled in their position, sometimes without even being asked.

Finally, a few Do's and Don't's:

Do	Don't
Call them Darling	Refer to them as servants
Be very clear when asking them to do something	Forget to pay them or else they get grumpy
Help them (or at least offer to help them) if they're carrying a lot of things	Ever give the impression they're not trusted, but don't trust them too much
Encourage them to marry each other; there's nothing quite so tender as a breeding pair	Leave them in the car on a hot day without opening a window
Praise and pat them when they do well	Patronise them too obviously
Decorate them at Christmas	Make them wear an unflattering uniform
Encourage them to wash	Threaten them with sticks

Step 2: One's Social Situation: Company and the company One keeps

One really cannot choose to whom One is related, but One can and should choose to whom One relates. Humankind should see society and sociability as great boons which distract One's attention away from the dark, crushing, inevitable knowledge that all who live eventually must die. Yes, rather than sitting at home spiralling downward, downward, ever downward towards the black light, invite some friends around. Better still, visit them in their own homes. Now, for friends to really 'work', One has to find friends with whom One has a lot in common. There's little sense in befriending some One who is Sportistic if One simply couldn't care less about sportism; it will lead to extended quiet patches in conversation and an uncomfortable atmosphere. Instead, make a positive effort to find Posh friends with whom One may talk gaily of Posh things. Or better still …

How to catch Posh friends

If only some One were to invent some sort of trap or lure to catch Posh friends, it would make it all so very much easier. But, without the aid of an entrapment device, Posh friends have to be caught the old-fashioned way: with charm, with money, with a smiley wink or with an Edwardian butterfly net.

Now, one of the disadvantages of Posh people is that they are so very nice to every One, it's easy to feel One's self singled out for friendship. The best thing to do is to approach the Posh person One may have singled out for friendship gently, giving an air of casual but only slight interest. Then, after the Posh person has lowered their guard and begun to show tender signs of trust – STRIKE. Any local library will have books on the delicacies of entrapping impala in the wild. Posh people are very similar to this – some even have identical musk-secreting glands and small, curly horns.

How to keep Posh friends

Keeping Posh friends is a delightful and rewarding pastime. These gentle, noble people need so very little direct maintenance – although One does have to commit to high levels of behavioural loveliness and a wardrobe of infinite distraction to keep their interest and friendship engaged. Other than trying so very hard to be Posh One's self, little else is required. However, sleight of hand, trained monkeys, spoon bending or other such amusements can go a long way to cultivating loyalty from One's friends. And if that fails, use money to buy them.

How to get rid of the Posh friends One has caught when One finds Posher friends

The secret is to try ever so hard not to be too brutal. Approach this trickiest of tricky situations with a gentle heart and perhaps some fabulously lovely presents to act as keepsakes of your former friendship. Or if a degree of tough love requires a more forceful stance because they're simply not getting the message, stick them into a cat skin and take them to a myopic vet to be put to sleep. For ever.

Step 3: One's Family Situation: Un-Posh Relatives

Imagine polishing One's life, One's environment, One's friends and One's self to a pitch of shiny sheeniness, only to be brutally brought down on aggregate by One's un-Posh family.

The Posh, being generally charming, dashing and polite, often find themselves with un-Posh friends. Indeed, the naughtier Posh indulge themselves frightfully in this way – making a point of collecting about them a deeply un-Posh social circle in the centre of which they can shine: a very edgy pursuit known as Poshing-down, which your kindly Authors refuse to endorse (unless of course money or a minor European title changes hands). But choosing One's friends, Posh or un-Posh, is one thing. Coping with One's family, Posh or un-Posh, is another. More than anything else, un-Posh relatives aren't passive; they do really go out of their nasty, ugly ways to be deeply and unattractively, actively un-Posh. They plot and plan to create and contrive situations of deep-vein embarrassment to humiliate Posher kin, a pursuit in which they take spiteful pleasure, particularly in public places such as the Ritz, where One's kindly taken them for lunch, or at One's cocktail parties, to which they have not been invited but have come anyway (despite their photographs being issued to the bouncers).

The un-Posh are hideously reliable at being hideous. On seeing any One or anything civilised, they will do all in their foetid self-bothering power to bring down, besmirch and ruinate all that's so very lovely in life. But all is not lost, there are solutions to hand.

Un-Posh relatives and how to find uses for them

Imperial Rome under the Caesars was a fabulously accommodating place for any One afflicted by un-Posh relatives who either stood as an obstacle in the line of succession, refused to marry their own sister, smelt bad or failed to co-ordinate their toga tassels with the new wall paintings. Scrolls and scrolls were inscribed with the decorous details of relative disposal. These days, since the unnecessarily intrusive invention of forensic science (and, indeed, the police force), One has to be more subtle.

PUTTING THEM ON THE PAYROLL works relatively well, although it is best not to expect them to provide any kind of value for money. One needs to create the right kind of role – clock-winder, gong-fermer, boot-blacker or simply ballast on a long voyage.

BUYING A FOREIGN TITLE for unpleasant, untalented, un-Posh relatives has made the aristocracy of continental Europe all that it is today. Consult www.titlesrus.com

AN IRON MASK, a remote tower and thou: there's something so deeply romantic about immurement and, of all the ways to prune the family tree, it's lovely to opt for so literary a solution. Also, of course, there's the budget option, requiring the application of an iron mask only. Contact a neighbourhood blacksmith or welding company.

GARDEN ORNAMENTATION can be expensive, so why not use un-Posh relatives who have an ability to stand still for long periods as statues. An important tip is to make sure they're far on the horizon, at the end of a long *allée* of trees or atop the pinnacle of a roof so that they have no chance to engage One's guests in any sort of conversation. One may also consider hiring them to occupy One's friends' hermitages.

DENIAL is the most simple method of all and has been buffed to a fine art by the British gentry over many generations.

SECTIONING is really the contemporary counterpart to immurement or the charming Venetian practice of paying a religious order to imprison an un-*Posh* relative for the rest of their natural life. There is, be warned, rather a lot of paperwork attached to sectioning these days, which is dull beyond belief but necessary. For a truly successful campaign, aim to convince the un-*Posh* relative themselves (as well as the authorities) of their mental inadequacies. There are obviously a thousand and one ways of achieving this, varying in many degrees of subtlety, but the simplest and still the best is to invisibly stitch their discarded clothes to the bedroom carpet each evening, which creates levels of hilarious frustration as they try to dress. For an added twist, urinate in their kettle just before the relative in question makes a cup of tea.

So What is the Situation?

Thank the lovely Lord of all *Posh* things, because it is now well and truly official; One really doesn't need to rely on One's situation to define One any longer. Hurrah! Being lumbered with a family of specific class or a job of particular purpose needn't be a hindrance in life nor indeed any kind of help, because today's reality requires One to just get on with being One.

And a particularly important part of being One is the impact One's lovely Onedom has on One's surroundings. So, therefore, Dear Reader, read on.

CHAPTER FIVE

One's Location

The Posh Home

It can be diverting, surprising – even amusing – to see the Posh at large. But to really feel the full effect of their consummate loveliness, seeing them in their own environment is rewarding beyond measure – although seeing the Posh without their clothes on comes a close second; in fact, it sometimes comes a close first.

The Posh can light up and literally gild their surroundings simply from the lovely reflection of their own loveliness. But then, like the restless sun itself, they pass on, leaving naught but shadow behind them. Remember the Legend of the Nymph Anaglypta (who was credited by the Ancient Greeks with the invention of wallpaper as she traced the shadow of her departing lover Apollo all over what would now be known as a 'feature wall'), which illustrates just how a Posh interior relies on the Posh actually being in it. So it makes sense really to try and harness some of that gorgeous ephemeral incandescence and create a permanent environment which those less Posh may also enjoy.

Having a Posh home is terribly, terribly important. It must be seen (however irksome and bothersome the commitment) as a necessity, since, in many communities, the shining example of a Posh home is all too horribly rare. But what does a Posh home look like? Is it a quite easily spotted temple to loveliness with miraculous statuary and a neatly combed gravel drive the length of Park Avenue? Does the bath water arrive in the bath via the solid-gold lips of smiling mermaids? Perhaps the four posts of the four-poster bed are intricately fashioned from solid blocks of rock crystal which have been turned and shaped to look like the four most beautiful humans in the history of humandom?

Well, that would be a reasonably good start. The home of the *Posh* is a lair of such loveliness that the sordid business of ordinary living loses all relevance, importance and meaning. There are countless stories of mere mortals blundering unforewarned through the doors of a *Posh* home never to speak reason again. And for bailiffs, whose sordid and detested role on this planet is to take away furniture One inadvertently forgets to pay for, the professional risks of being sent to a *Posh* house to pursue their bestial purpose are obvious. Folklore is replete with tales of bailiffs unable to resist the siren call of the very home they were sent to take away found several decades later in understairs cupboards, trouser presses or priest holes, having reverted to a feral state. Indeed, some have been known to live undetected as footmen.

Posh on the outside: Front doors, door bells and getting away with net curtains (well, almost)

In ages past, the front door was aggressively studded and cross braced with iron as a statement of exclusivity and antisociability. Today, even the suburbs are replete with hefty oak doors blinged up with scowling door knockers depicting the likeness of dyspesic lions with improbably large rings in their snarling mouths. Indeed, the look for much of the twentieth century seems to have been 'scary baronial', an unfriendly style and deeply unsuccessful even when perpetrated by scary barons. The message to the rest of the world was: 'If the wrought iron gate fails to snatch your fingers, then the concrete lions standing sentinel at the porch will have your nose off.'

Recently, effort has been made to soften the face One's house presents to the planet with 'designer details' such as galvanised steel planters rather than lead, prairie grass rather than hedging and a split-level jumble of raked gravel and blue-painted decking as a replacement to the in/out drive. Ultimately, this contemporary approach is doomed, since the house itself remains the sullen suburban box it always was and a jaunty, purple painted door merely makes matters worse.

No, the outside of One's house should be like the expensively discreet wrappings of a Bond Street jeweller. Make One's exterior orderly and dignified, kindly condescending even. Lacquer black is the perfect and polite colour for a front door (polite since One's callers may check their reflection in its mirror like perfection), whilst front-door bells are to be avoided since they sound either too electrically urgent or (sin of sins) have pretensions to melody.

It is also worth noting that house names rather than numbers present a minefield for the uninitiated. Generally speaking, a house name that is not followed by a description of the structure, as in 'House', 'Lodge', 'Cottage' or 'Palace', may seem pretentious, but then there's nothing *more* pretentious than a cottage masquerading as a 'lodge', a sprawling pseudo-Tudor ranch fit for a glamour model calling itself a 'mansion' or a draughty, badly decorated London abode being known as 'Buckingham Palace'.

And as for net curtains? Only with bucketfuls of irony and a wry understanding that, from the out-side, an acreage of nylon lace does for the aesthetics of the house the same job it does for One's granny when she's feeling a little 'loved up'.

The ideal home:
A checklist for an adorable abode

* A portcullis
* Plenty of room for entertaining, a ballroom or two would do
* Parking for two yachts
* A glass elevator
* Turrets
* A kitchen full of kitchen things, including a spaniel-powered spit
* A long drive
* A long walk to the loo
* Nice views from the bath
* A nice view of the bath
* A grand staircase
* A ghost or two, including a malevolently camp poltergeist with a penchant for East-meets-West fusion furniture layouts
* Ivy growing on the inside walls
* An odd smell
* Lots of mirrors (anything to flatter), including a mirrored ceiling
* A 'For Sale' sign (useful but not essential)
* A dungeon
* A torture chamber
* A tortoise chamber (and rooms for all One's pets)
* A sitting tenant
* Staff accommodation
* Staff
* A bedroom
* A roof
* Some floors

Do bear in mind that, for a properly Posh home, One would require a minimum of nineteen of the above.

Posh Areas: Gorgeous ghettos

Posh areas are quite literally where a lot of Posh people live. They are not that easy to identify, it must be admitted. Posh people, as they are so attractive and ornamental, aren't often at home (their calendars are full months in advance). So finding a Posh area through dogged surveillance is time consuming and requires many sleepless nights sitting in a car with binoculars and a Thermos of milky coffee (although do resist the temptation to fill One's Thermos with half-caf latte, since the Posh have sensitive nostrils and are put off by the merest whiff of pretentious coffee). In fact, finding badger setts on motorway lay-bys is easier – particularly since showy, rich areas (with which Posh areas really mustn't be confused) are easily spotted from outer space and can be terribly, terribly distracting.

Generally speaking, Posh areas will have some kind of hub or focus that drew the Posh to the area in the first place. Marvellous, unexpected shops full of low-key lovely things or indeed shining views of some architectural wonder will nearly always inspire a close knit colony of breeding Posh to roost. But One shouldn't forget that, since the Posh are so deeply disinterested in money things, property values are often unexpectedly low, which means the area itself is rather mixed.

Here for the curious reader, there follows a few pointers to ascertaining the *Posh* rating of any area:

* Does the area have 'Royal Borough of' before it? (Un-*Posh*)
* Does the area have gondolas? (*Posh*)
* Does the area have large gates, an electric fence, sentry boxes and big rabid dogs? (Un-*Posh*, unless it is a prison)
* Does the area have a lot of busy, marvellous shops full of unexpected and exciting trifles staffed by friendly well-dressed shop people? (*Posh*)
* Does the area have noble trees lining its streets? (*Posh*)
* Does the area have Ignoble dog eggs studding its pavements? (Un-*Posh*)
* Does the area have a large concrete shopping centre? (Un-*Posh*)
* Does the area induce wide-eyed surprise when One asks a taxi driver to take One there? (*Posh*)
* Does the area inspire slack-jawed greed when One asks a taxi driver to take One there? (Un-*Posh*)
* Does the driver speed off without letting One in when One asks a taxi driver to take one there? (see *Posh* pioneers, following page)
* Do wealthy Sportists inhabit the area? (Un-*Posh*)
* Do wealthy prostitutes inhabit the area? (*Posh*)
* Does the area have regular rubbish collections? (Un-*Posh* and *Posh*)
* Do people use elephants as transport in the area? (*Posh*)
* Do the less wealthy people in the area dress in pearl buttons, sing songs about 'a bamboo' and dance? (*Posh*)
* Do the middling wealthy all play golf at once? (Un-*Posh*)
* Is human sacrifice practised in the area? (Normally, Un-*Posh*)
* Does the area ooze loveliness? (*Posh, Posh, Posh, Posh, Posh*)

Posh pioneers: Living a lovely life in a no-go area

Far from huddling together for shared protection (a very un-Posh way of living forever associated with the rich), the Posh are constantly adventurous in their choice of habitat. It's thanks to the Posh, not the gentry, that areas become 'gentrified', as estate-mongers say.

For an eighteenth-century façade, a Regency wrought iron porch in the chinoiserie style or ornately scrolled stucco so bold and rich it looks like icing, the Posh will move anywhere. Regardless of the malodorous knots of scowling hoodies, heroin addicts, upturned supermarket trollies and breeze tossed carrier bags blown in constant tarantellas by the sulphurous wind fresh from the gasworks. No, the Posh see all of that sort of ugliness as ugliness that really can't help itself and, like vigorous Victorian missionaries, they view even the hoody in its aggressive sportswear as an opportunity for loveliness waiting to happen. By and large, and thanks to their wonderful self-confidence and infectious evangelical commitment to making the world a lovely place, Posh people are quickly welcomed into even the roughest areas with open arms. They are rarely robbed or mugged – although random acts of frenzied frotterism are not unknown in shadowed alleys.

Slumming it

Slumming it can be fun. It means, quite literally, living in a slum by choice rather than income embarrassment. To do slumming, One needs to:

* Have a driveway less than half a mile long (believe it or not there are such homes)
* Have no more than one house
* Have the same number of bedrooms (or fewer) as people who live there
* Have a front room
* Have no form of gatehouse whatsoever
* Have wheels on the bottom of the house (this is known as a 'caravan')
* Have no columns anywhere at all (impossible in Essex, where all columns go to die)
* Have a bus stop close by
* Have a view of other people's land beyond the land owned by One
* Have no room to swing a cat. Nor a kitten, sometimes

Buying Posh Homes Poshly

Once One has found the area in which One wants to live, One must then set about finding the perfect home in which to put One's lovely things.

Estate-mongers: A dirty inevitability

Bizarrely, even areas of the most piratical roughness have their own estate-mongers lurking furtively in the undergrowth. Despite the impression that One could swap a comb or the sparkly fragments of mirror and a bird whistle with the locals in exchange for a derelict but gorgeous Georgian townhouse, inevitably, before the transaction may be completed, an estate-monger will swoop. Stepping gingerly from a darkly armoured German car, the smarmy bugger will insist on taking a cut.

Remember: estate-mongers are not *born* but most certainly *made*. Once upon a time, they had mummies and daddies, possibly even pets and/or playground chums. So the knack is to try and penetrate the thickened crust of sulphurous evil and appeal to a better them. Good bloody luck.

Estate-mongers (ever in their slyness) go on and on about property being more than bricks and mortar and that buying and selling a house is very emotional. Not for them, for they have no emotions, oh, no, not a one. But for purchasers and purchasettas, or vendors and vendettas, the whole process can become abominably fraught. And that is just what the estate-mongers want. To heighten their twisted pleasure, they'll often call in an equally malevolent mate who is a solicitor and who has a university degree in 'twisting the knife' along with stylised depictions of the 178 families he enjoyed making homeless last year painted on the side of his shiny black car. So be warned, armour One's self against all of this, show no fear or perturbation, no chink in that armour. Then turn the tables by insisting on negotiating only in either guineas or krugerrands.

Moving and moving in

Moving-in day is terribly important. If your neighbours have net curtains, they'll be twitching a lot in an effort to catch a glimpse of the new arrivals.

A useful tip is to pack One's things so that One's most beautiful objects (Sèvres overmantel clocks, petit point fire screens, shellwork chandeliers or One's collection of limited-edition hand-painted twenty-two-carat-gold-edged plates depicting the favoured fast food outlets of the late Elvis Presley) are at the top of the tea chest. Below them, out of sight, may be transported the dull practicalities of daily life like vacuum cleaners, loo seats, children.

With new neighbours, at the faintest rustle of net curtainage, wave vigorously and smile electrically in their direction. It will soon shame them into breaking cover and revealing themselves, ensuring One demonstrates that, despite One's gorgeous glory, One intends to be an interested and energetic neighbour. They may even bake you a nice pie.

Always ensure that table lamps, light bulbs and scented candles are easily found. The first evening in a new home is very important and can be made lovely by having the right lighting at One's disposal.

Dealing with tradesmen (without sounding pre-war)

The excitement of the first few days in One's new home carries with it new and diverting opportunities to call in professionals who are experts in the colour of rooms, erecting conservatories, making two rooms into one or, that most mysterious of mystical concepts, re-wiring.

Tradesmen dealing in these trades (known collectively as 'builderators') tend to be bluff characters with large pink faces and extremely tight rolls of paper, very mushy at one end and alight at the other, which they smoke.

The secret with builderators is: write absolutely everything down. In fact, builderators need lists like cups need saucers (speaking of which, they can become inexplicably paralysed if they don't drink enough sugar in their tea).

They have a hugely specialised vocabulary and a dialect that renders all words that end in 't' t-less and all words that would ordinarily start 'th' to start with 'f' instead. And, by the way, 'th's at the end of words become 'v's.

It can be confusing, but take the time to refer to the builderator/English dictionary below:

A LONG WEIGHT – a poor joke at the expense of junior builderators, who are sent to the shop for 'a long wait' (Ha, ha, ha)

ARCHITRAY – the wooden moulding around a door (architrave)

CHIPPY – One who chips away at wood hoping eventually to make a shelf

DROPPING THE KIDS OFF AT THE POOL – a much looked forward to mid-morning activity that requires a tabloid newspaper

FLUSH (as in 'the loo') – an activity all builderators see as pointless

IT'S A BIGGER JOB THAN THOUGHT – builderators often confuse the word 'bigger' and the term 'more expensive'

MDF – 'Massive Dance Fenomena', a pop group popular with builderators

PHWOOAAR – a polite way of greeting a lady's breasts

PONCEY (semi-disparaging) – anything that's not a brick or a nail

ROLLIE REGATTA – the jolly, sporty sight of an extremely over-ripe, unflushed loo on whose meniscus abandoned roll-up cigarette butts bob and jostle as in the opening race at the Henley Royal Regatta

SLAG – a term of considerable affection used about more or less any One

SPARKY – One of a particularly morose and unhelpful disposition who, in the act of making the electricity work in one room, ensures that the rest of the street is in darkness

SPLASH – an amount of milk in their sugar dissolved in hot tea

SPLOSH – sugar dissolved in hot tea

TOILET – loo

Thus, fore-armed with the previous, One may go into negotiation with builderators without a perpetual look of charmed befuddlement which any builderator will take to mean that money is no object and that they're currently engaged in a conversation with a being they like to refer to as a 'sucker'.

Decorating Poshly

Traditionally, those who were of a sort who didn't know how to decorate a house nicely called in a charming gentleman known as a Poshterior Decorator. His marvellous eye and surgically enhanced taste would be able to transform the meanest of mansions into a statement of such exquisite and rarefied Poshness that the mere proximity to such perfection was beyond ocular orgasm. Sadly, Poshterior Decorators are expensive, exclusive and unavailable from May to November, as they have a frightful migrating habit. So One has to do 'DIO', or Design It One's Self.

Setting the tone in your new Posh home

Obviously, Posh is as Posh does, so the Posh home can more or less be made to accommodate all manner of personal home decorating statements. That said, there are several items of interior embellishment which are currently all the rage but which require more effort to make work Poshly:

CROCHET is by its nature see-through, which makes it fabulously exciting when turned into ladies' jump-suits or gentlemen's waistcoats but useless in the home for any form of concealment. Crochet can, however, be used to make intriguing room dividers that ooze olde worlde charm.

STUFFED AND MOUNTED HEADS come in a terribly restricted range of colours, which makes them useless for colour accenting. They do, however, lend a certain grandeur to larger, more high-ceilinged spaces. A clever tip is to install remote controlled eyeballs so that their gaze may, quite literally, follow One around the room. Fur-bearing mammals are traditionally popular for stuffing and mounting, but there has been a recent trend for displaying other mammals instead, such as Canadians.

MINIMALISM is, technically speaking, a really very silly idea indeed. Still, if One's set One's heart on it, then the secret with minimalism is to throw away everything One owns and spend the evenings sitting staring at a light switch.

IRON AGE tastes in interior decoration were, to say the least, brutalist, which is perhaps why this look is beginning to catch on amongst young urban office workers. The central fire pit with corresponding ceiling hole is convenient and eye-catching.

20 things One should never share One's location with

There are, lurking in the dark corners of existence, a collection of interior embellishments of such bestial repulsion they should never even be considered for inclusion in One's home.

These include:

* A five-piece three-piece suite
* Antimacassars (even in irony)
* Fibreglass carpet tiles
* Some One else's excrement
* Barbed wire
* Scatter cushions with pie crust edging
* Depictions of vintage cars made from clock parts mounted on black velvet
* Jolly homeless people made from porcelain on onyx occasional tables
* Scratch-and-sniff wall coverings
* Cut crystal bowls filled with boiled sweets
* Anything bearing the term 'BritArt'
* Shop dummies wearing clown wigs
* Polystyrene ceiling tiles
* Internal combustion engines
* Pre-Raphaelite paintings in ornate frames
* Colour-changing fibre-optic Christmas trees
* Sofa beds
* Bad smells
* Absolutely anything at all displayed in a clip frame
* Horse brasses

Not to mention pink toilet suites, plastic slipcovers, glow-in-the-dark ceiling stickers, inflatable furniture or anything animatronic.

Gardening in the Gnome Counties: A design-free zone

There are those of a sort who are known for their delusions of blandeur and for whom gardens are seen as appropriate environments for the following extraordinary items:

* A miniature golf course
* A crazy golf course
* A collection of crazy conifers
* A mentalist golf course *with* a collection of crazy conifers
* Crazy paving
* Carriage lamps
* A wishing well
* Topiary self-portraits of all the family
* A mass grave
* A funfair
* A sweat lodge
* The world in miniature
* A Travel Lodge
* A crop circle

Home is Where the Tart is

The home environment has always been such a marvellous context for the lovely display of Posh things and Poshness in general. Over the centuries, mankind has effected a change to Poshkind, thanks to the clever installation of lacquered panels with gilded corner details, architectonic cushions stuffed with bumfluff and motorised crystal chandeliers that play country on a whim. The embellishment of One's home is a fine art that all should be proud to exercise. And, indeed, once One has successfully re-wrought One's location in One's image through the medium of aesthetic scent-making, why, then it's time to have some fun.

CHAPTER SIX

One's Recreation

The Things One Gets up to in Between Being Onederful

Recreation was invented by the Ancient Romans as a cure for boredom. It was a way of diverting and amusing the *Posh* end of the populace in an effort to fill the time between Punic wars. Pretty soon, recreation became a real craze and, as the gap between the wars got longer (in fact it's been a few thousand years since the last one, so we must be due another soon), recreation became the only thing that the peoples of rank and money actually did all day. This meant that the four great categories of recreation – entertaining, shopping, culturism and sportism – became fabulously developed, with rich sociological histories and enticing traditions of their very own. This resulted in the invention of special ways of communicating and some very, very unusual outfits.

Thus, until relatively recently, recreation was all the rich and the lovely ever did. No One had a job or, indeed, 'had' to work. Recreation was an all engrossing pursuit very much in its own right. But now it's different, alas. Recreation has to be shoe-horned in between all One's other commitments, such as earning money, visiting relatives, picking up the dry cleaning, being summoned to appear in court and doing sex.

Wrong recreating

As discussed above, thanks to the creative flair of the elegantly toga'd Romans, we today recognise four great tributaries which converge to swell the mighty cataract of eddying loveliness that is the river of recreation. But along the way, as so often happens when humankind is left to its own devices, other forms of recreation were invented by strangely sociophobic people who occupied the very, very fringes of society. Please avoid recreating in the following ways at all costs:

HOBBIES – the word 'hobby' derives from an ancient Abyssinian term meaning 'weird and friendless twat'. Hobbies are ways of recreating which are so very engrossing and consuming for the hobbyist concerned that attention may be diverted away from the cruel and bitter inadequacies in their hollow and tortuously unfulfillable lives. Hobbies cover a wide and satanically dark palette of poisonous activities.

CRAFT – 'hobby' and 'craft' are the kind of words that sit successfully together in a mired besmirchment of complacent ghastliness. People who craft will often drape themselves with their craft like ugly, fat Christmas trees.

SPOTTING THINGS – should really be useful and interesting, such as spotting the world's loveliest Corinthian columns for the eventual publication of a slim volume illustrated with One's own insightful drawings. But to spot airplanes or trains or buses or, worst of all, ferries demonstrates an almost sectionable mentality of a level normally only achieved by oatmeal.

BREEDING THINGS – mucking around with genetics in emulation of God was seized upon by malodorous, friendless hobbyists early on as an ultimately impotent attempt at righting the wrongs in their futile lives. The idea is to take something perfectly usable, like a dahlia or a lap dog, and muck it around using tweezers to take seed from the one to transfer to the egg of the other and generally pervert the course of natural selection.

Then, when they are left with alarmingly useless bundles of cells which look ridiculous and smell bad, they then show them off in a public arena.

COLLECTING THINGS – Being known as a 'collector' sounds grand and rather distinguished. And, as a pursuit, collecting may indeed be both grand and distinguished, providing One's collection is a collection of grand and distinguished things. Collections of *Star Trek* memorabilia, surgical shoes, Smurfs, milk-bottle tops, bobble hats, tufts, wire coat-hangers or contemporary art are a sign of an unusually pointless personality.

And so, having plumbed the depths, let us now rise like an unhindered champagne bubble up to the light to study the right forms of recreation, otherwise known as the four elegant pillars.

The First Pillar: Shopping

Buying things for pleasure is a cornerstone of *Posh*. The whole process of shopping brings with it countless opportunities for engorgeousness, for amusement and for glamorous diversion. The truly *Posh*, such as our waterlily-borne Authors, can shop absolutely anywhere, turning the simple, basic act of exchanging a few copper coins for a hand-embroidered toothpick purse of softened and dyed yak skin into a fine art. In fact, it is just such off-road retail purchases which provide an almost post-coital thrill difficult to match in a glitzy purpose-built shiny shop. But, like all fine arts, shopping carries with it a few rules of perspective, the most important of which is to avoid anything that might refer to itself as a yard sale, car boot sale, missed sale or indeed sale sale.

What to buy and where to buy it

There are certain things One really shouldn't buy, since they are not Posh. If there are things One really has to have in One's life – such as sock suspenders, drawer liners, denture adhesive, dog chews or iron reinforcing bars – One should explore shopping by an Internet, which is secret and very private. If One doesn't have an Internet, then send out One's household staff. But for all other lovely things – shop till One drops.

As something of a public service, our enormous-hearted Authors have compiled the following thumbnail sketch (and what lovely thumbnails, by the way) of what to buy and from where.

What to buy…	and from where
Fruit and Vegetables	The floating market in Bangkok or, failing that, Fortnum and Masons
Hairbrushes	Mason Pearson
Ladies' Umbrellas	Chantal Thomas
Ladies' Under-things	Open Cast Engineering Corporation of Taipei factory outlet
Rubber Tyres	Honest Pierre's Tyres – 68 Rue de Rue, Poitiers
Gaily Coloured Gloves	Glove-a-gogo, Sta Maoise, Venice
Fine Bone China	Any shiny shop

Avoiding bargains

It really is so very important for One's self-respect to avoid bargains. Bargains are cheap, and their cheapness is their only point. Occasionally, One finds One's self in the tricky position of seeing a thing in a shop One really deeply wants to own but, when One enquires its price, One discovers to One's horror that it's actually rather inexpensive. This happens a lot in supermarkets, where things like tins of baked beans are sold for virtually no money whatsoever. So should One be so very unlucky as to come across a cheap object One can't escape from wanting, haggle. Offer twice the price. One owes it to One. (And, of course, you, Dear Purchaser of this elegantly informative volume, insisted on paying double its elegantly published price. In guineas.)

Another testing annoyance of contemporary life is a free thing. One can be in a perfectly nice, perfectly reputable shop buying something, only to find there is an 'offer of specialness', or some such foolishness, which means One is given a free thing. Free things (as in things One gives no money for) rarely have any aesthetic merit and are usually only given away free because no One in their right mind wants to buy them. Also, beware 'buy one, get one free'. One would have thought that to avoid getting one free when One bought one, all One would do would be to buy two. But no. What happens then is that One gets two free as well as the two ones One's bought in the first place.

And, be warned, shops occasionally write SALE all over their windows. One really must, at whatever the personal cost, not go into a shop with SALE written all over the windows. The word SALE means 'things that don't fit or that don't smell right and that cost very little money now they've been well and truly fingered by Tom, Dick *and* Harry, or that have been tried on by a coach-load of dumpy women who've taken the dark art of under-grooming to new depths of bestial unpleasantness'.

People who sell things: An unusual breed

People who sell things to One in shops are part of a rich, historical cavalcade of tradition. Indeed, it was the Emperor Napoleon who suggested that the British are a 'Nation of Shopkeepers', which is quite funny really, since the British are actually a 'Nation of Binary-Speaking Computer Analysts and Deep-Fat Fryers'. Our shopkeepers and shop assistants are the very cream of cream of our British society, as they do a job of great social importance in the cause of *Poshness*. In fact, there would be a 'people who work in shops day', if it were not for the inescapable fact the shops would have to shut for it, which would be most disastrous.

People who work in the shiniest of shiny shops are designed to be quite rude. They have to stand on very reflective marble floors all day, which doesn't help their mood. Ordinary people often misconstrue this sharpness of tone. For like the three-headed guardian of the gates of hell, Cerberus, people who work in shiny shops are there to ensure that un-*Posh* people don't buy any of their lovely, shiny things. Which makes sense. But it is therefore of paramount importance that One's *Poshness* is so very obvious when One goes shopping in shiny shops. In fact, One mustn't see the wearing of tiaras or even coronets as a step too far.

Ordinary, interesting-things shops tend to be looked after by more ordinary, interesting people who have an interest in the sort of things they sell. What's lovely is when interesting-things shops all huddle together to make interesting streets to shop in. Greenwich Village in New York is like this, as is South Molton Street in London and Le Place des Choses d'Interesting in Paris.

Shops that are as big as aircraft hangars are bewildering places to shop unless One is truly dedicated. They give One a really rather clever, cart-like wire chariot on rather bossy wheels, which One can fill with whopping shopping. Although they do like One to give the chariot back at the end unless One passes an urban canal, in which case One may park them upsidedown in the water. The people who sell things in these shops are deliberately bewildered people who are trained not to know their arse from their elbow.

Changing rooms: An underused resource

Most shops (apart from shops as large as aircraft hangars) have changing rooms or little cubicles with a curtain across the front which One may borrow for fifteen minutes or so at a time. These darkened little spaces are for taking off One's clothes and then putting on others to see if One would like to buy them. But there are other things to do in the warm, quiet privacy behind that heavy curtain:

* have a nap
* have a nip
* have a lovely long look at One's unfettered finery in the full length mirror
* catch up on One's reading
* try on clothes backwards
* fart in quiet comfort
* wee in the corner (gentlemen only)
* practise humming
* picnic with a friend
* do colouring-in
* do sex with a friend
* burrow through to the next changing room using a nail file smuggled in inside a small layer cake

Shopping without paying

Although carrying cash can be such a bore, it is nonetheless traditional to pay money for the things One buys, and this is called shopping. Not paying money for what One buys is called shoplifting, and shoplifting, for some reason, makes people cross. So, should One wish to give shoplifting a go, then do try hard not to be caught by people when doing it.

Posh shoplifting

There are several ways to shoplift *Poshly*. Smaller, easily palmed items such as diamond rings, engraved gems, antique coins or boiled sweets may be slipped discreetly inside a glove. Long, thin objects *de virtu* – Jacobean ceremonial dress swords, tubes of oil paint or battery-driven appliances of feminine enjoyment – may be stealthily slid within the folds of a loosely furled umbrella. And why not borrow a trick or two from the Ottoman court of eighteenth-century Istanbul and affect a janissary's turban of such prodigious size, a flat screen TV with DVD player may be completely concealed in its generous swaggage.

Posh solutions to common shopping problems

Without doubt, the most common shopping problem is parking. *Posh* parking is the ideal answer and hinges on the simplest of simple premises: that no matter how many parking tickets, court orders, clamps or towaway trucks One has to pay for because One has left One's car with the hazard lights flashing on a pavement right outside the shop One's shopping in, it's still going to cost far less than engaging a full-time chauffeur, based on the calculation that chauffeurs cost around about three-quarters of a million pounds a year to run.

Another problem which One may encounter is an inability to pay for the shopping One wants. Obviously, as just previously discussed, shoplifting is One solution but sometimes One simply doesn't have an opportunity for that kind of forethought. No, sometimes One finds that, quite unbeknownst to One, One's credit card has run out of whatever it is that makes it work. This can be most embarrassing, principally for the person who works in the shop, who has to confront One with the dreaded news.

Then there's the knotty problem of what to do should One discover One doesn't actually like One's shopping when One gets it home. Apparently, One may swap One's unwanted shopping in return for money. But, quite frankly, is the shame of having shopped so badly in the first place worth mere money? One thinks not. So, just recycle any shopping own-goals in the direction of One's household staff – they'll see them as perks.

The next illustrious, much celebrated and flavourful way of recreating is culturising.

The Second Pillar: Culture (The Posh heroin)

Culture is addictive, anti-social and peddled by gentlemen in wide brimmed hats made of plush in various bright colours. They have no conscience or remorse for the families they split or the lives they ruin. In fact, there are times when One has to see the un-Posh as lucky to be unsusceptible to the siren call of that hollow-cheeked-sap-sucking-mistress, Madame Culture.

To have not developed an unquenchable thirst for the string sound of Purcell, to have no unswervable longing for the blues of a Cimabue altarpiece and to have never developed spiritual bulimia from long-term exposure to opera – ah, how the unlettered and unmannered have escaped the perpetual auto-sadism of feeling far too deeply!

Culture comes in a variety of different packages, each lovelier than the one before and all offering to stimulate every single one of One's erogenous zones at once. Divine never-ending torture.

Music: Aural sex

By what satanic alchemy the very air around One is coaxed to vibrate, quiver and shudder in waves of ambrosial melody is just one of those mysteries to which One simply doesn't want to have a prosaic answer.

For the *Posh*, whose very souls are made from all the raw nerve endings God had left over after he'd finished making angels, music is a trial of ecstasy. And the *Posh*, being so very *Posh*, have an ability to find a little grain of beauty in even the most brutal of musical noises. Bless 'em.

Listening to *Posh* music *Poshly*

Listening to *Posh* music can be something of an ordeal for the un-*Posh*. There are just so very, very, very many notes, each more perfectly rounded than the one before. Without the appropriate receiving and unscrambling equipment, it's not hard to imagine the sort of mess Mozart makes of the heads of the common. So, it's no surprise the fleshy ears of the brutish have so tough a time of it. To help those not born with the right kind of aural or cultural equipment, please feel most free to refer to the following instructions for how to listen to *Posh* music; it will help One feel more at home with high culture.

* Sit down on a chair
* Get comfortable (feel free to skibble around, cross and uncross One's legs, fold and unfold One's arms until relaxed state is achieved)
* Don't tense (tensing will do you no favours in the long term)
* Resist the temptation to giggle (*Posh* music often sounds rather eccentric and atonal. This is known as 'warming up')
* Park your eyeballs on something neutral and not too diverting at a reasonably high level on a wall or low level on a ceiling
* Open your ears
* Moisten and part your lips slightly
* Prepare to receive music
* Receive music

It's all a lot simpler than One may have been led to believe. Now, if you have gone to a public music hall, after the music has finished there are often some nice drinks on offer in some lovely place with a lot of mirrors and ornate panelling. Whilst drinking, people may ask you what you felt about the experience. They may even use some foreign names, which are the names of composers. Here follows a lucid but swift skittle through the great composers and what their hit number ones were:

Composers — A Spotter's Guide

Vivaldi	Wrote most car adverts (amazing, since there are no cars in his home town of Venice). His music is often jolly energetic and should call to mind visual images such as storm clouds over the Veneto or swiftly jiggling private bits. Something of an ambassador for gingerkind.
Handel	Made a career out of writing the theme tune for 'Amen'. His real talent was to put as few as eight words to music and make them last for three hours.
Purcell	Was, unusually, British. His music is best listened to while wearing an enormously tall wig. It helps the acoustics, apparently.
Henry VIII	Wrote 'Greensleeves', which was originally called 'Greenteeth' but the first line, 'My Lady of the Greenteeth,' wasn't nice.
Bach	There were more than a few Bachs, which can confuse. All of them were good at Big music and one of them was brilliant at Small music.
Haydn	Wrote the German national anthem, inadvertently.
Mozart	Was as talented a composer as he was a chocolatier.
Mendelssohn	Had a sister called Fanny.

Composers — A Spotter's Guide

Schubert	Was a jovial-looking gentleman who wrote a charming piece of music about a trout, which is unusual.
Puccini	Made operas so very, very big that they have parts for elephants and camels and are often staged in footballerist arenas.
Tchaikovsky	Wrote the theme tune to Christmas. He had a rather unusual private life and was married to Glenda Jackson's doppelgänger.
Debussy	Is perfect to listen to on the French Riviera whilst cycling with a basket full of lavender and Femidoms over One's arm.
Gilbert and Sullivan	Were actually two people of Victorian persuasion who wrote jolly operas that were supposed to be rather funny.
Beethoven	Was not a nice fellow like Mozart and his music is rarely 'nice', although it is always, always, always beautiful. Beethoven invented jazz. And he fell out with Napoleon. Any music One recognises that is not by Mozart will probably be by Beethoven.
Stravinsky	Should be treated with great caution. Exciting stuff but tricky for the uninitiated: some of his note combinations have been scientifically proven to vibrate sphincters at dangerous speeds.
Bartók	Likewise Bartók, whose music can sound like a cat tied to a piano.
Elgar	Most beloved by all British people because of his Britishness and his British music, which makes all British people sing along and sway when they hear it – like friendless brass-rubbers.
Benjamin Britten	Was another British music writer. He had a very, very best friend called Peter, who sang very high indeed and had very crispy hair.
Dolly Parton	Universally acknowledged as the very best music. It's funny, sassy and sad all at the same time. Just like Dolly herself, who is very, very lovely indeed.

Listening to Un-Posh music Poshly

As discussed, the very Posh will find loveliness in everything around them. This includes nearly all music. But there are exceptions – Celine Dion, Bizet, Michael Bolton, anything *a capella* and solo harpsichord scats. Avoid these like a very catching plague.

Very un-Posh music that is surprisingly good includes Meatloaf, Cornish sea shanties, the score for *West Side Story*, Bryan Adams and some jazz. So One shouldn't feel distressed should One find One's self somewhere where the music of any of the above is being played.

Opera and ballet: An odd notion

The thing about both opera and ballet is that nobody speaks. But this is not a disadvantage, since opera and ballet come with lovely music, by and large, and ballet theatres and opera houses tend to be the loveliest buildings in the world. Just sitting there listening to music under crystal chandeliers of an almost algebraic complexity can be a near-divine experience.

If One had a gripe about opera singers, whilst being lovely people with lovely personalities, it is that they are often rather difficult to dress. And, when their character is supposed to be wasting away with consumption, it's a bit difficult to believe, since it's obvious it's been but a few short minutes since their last pie. Ballet dancers, however, are the reverse. And male balletists have an unusual compulsion to wear the tightest tights over their freakishly large thighs. For some reason or other, Lord knows why, they always have ceramic hubcaps down the very front of their trousers. Perhaps it's to protect their fineries from the roses people throw.

Theatre: An acquired taste and how to acquire it

'The theatre' is an expression One may roll around One's mouth, so it's worthwhile saying that One is 'going to the theatre' rather than 'going to see a play' (which is really all that One does when One goes to the theatre).

To be honest, One does have rather to watch out when going to the theatre – it can all go horribly wrong if One finds One's self at something too modern or too taxing. Further, since theatres aren't anything near as lovely as opera houses, there's less chance of a glamorous architectural distraction to entice.

To be fair on theatres, they do try to give One coded warnings with the large illuminated words they display outside which describe the production. So terms like 'lavish', 'opulent' and 'a visual feast' mean the play is, well, a visual feast and worth seeing if just for the frocks and scenery. Terms like 'challenging', 'unmissable' and 'a brave reworking' suggest something most unpleasant and indeed most missable.

On the upside, One can buy sweets or chocolates in cardboard boxes which, in this day and age, is most unusual. For those with a sweet tooth, going to the theatre, no matter how rubbish the play, is worth the experience. Besides, the occasional 'challenging' play requires the people in the play not to wear clothes, which is why One can hire little red binoculars for 50p.

Art: Posh porn

Nowhere is the gulf between Posh culture and un-Posh culture so very apparent than it is with art. Posh art is so very, very clever and beautiful and, most often, sexually arousing. Un-Posh art is, at its very best, deeply annoying and, at its very worst, enough to make One really quite angry. Things went horribly wrong in art in the twentieth century. Pablo Picasso was an artist who was very clever and also a terrible, terrible tease. He invented a marvellous joke he called Cubism, whereby he painted very, very badly indeed and on purpose and said that it was extremely modern to paint badly. Now, unbeknownst to Picasso, everybody in the world took his little jest seriously and, before long it all got out of hand. Then just look what happened …

By and large, it is best to avoid most bits of modern art, although modern art galleries are really very lovely buildings and often the most marvellous settings for drinks parties. There is a variety of Posh art to look out for. Here are just a few:

Art for Art's Sake — Art and What It's Called

Ancient Art	Very, very old indeed. Can be Egyptian or Greek.
Roman Art	Like Greek art, but less reliant on naked boys (which is probably a good thing).
Medieval Art	Charming for Christmas cards. Although, for some reason, medieval artists were much worse at art than Roman artists.
Renaissance Art	A Posh backlash against medieval art having gone a little wrong (even though it is very charming). Raphael was extremely good-looking whilst Michelangelo was a frightful under-groomer.
Mannerist Art	Made everyone very long and thin. Mannerist art was painted by gentlemen who were, in hindsight, not the marrying kind.

Art for Art's Sake — Art and What It's Called

Baroque Art	Was great fun indeed. Big and noisy paintings with very many flying people, like the better sort of Hollywood film.
Rococo Art	A lovely word. All about sweet paintings of pertly, pretty peasants who are obviously extremely happy in fluffy bits of nature.
Neo-Classical Art	Is most worthy and elevated in intent but very low on laughs.
Romantic Art	Was really just Baroque art coming back in. Even at the time, people thought it rather retro.
Pre-Raphaelite Art	Favoured very dark, sultry ladies with painfully swollen lips and the faintest hint of a moustache. Actually, not faint enough.
Impressionist Art	Is today highly prized for use on 'in deepest sympathy' cards.
Post-Impressionist Art	Describes a lot of things and different ways of doing art that came after the Impressionists but before the whole silly joke of modern art that naughty little Picasso accidentally invented.

Some notes on modern art

Although it is not all what One would call 'good', it can at least be decorative (One hopes), and comes in so many different flavours:

CUBISM – art the wrong way around

FUTURISM – art the wrong way around but at speed

DADA – art inside out

SURREALISM – art inside out and so plainly mad it's quite amusing (and fishy)

VORTICISM – lots and lots of vortexes

FAUVISM – big colours done with very big brushes indeed

ABSTRACT EXPRESSIONISM – looks marvellous in waiting rooms of banks

POP ART – pictures of soup tins

OP ART – pictures of vertigo

BRIT ART – pointless and expensive. Requires rubber gloves and disinfectant

Literature

Literature, since it comes in the shape of books, which are very handy and may be carried around with One, is extremely popular. Britain really invented literature. A lot of the best sort of art was done in Italy, a lot of the best sort of music was done in German places, but nearly all the best literature is British. It would be lovely at this point to think of something the French are good at.

Literature has the power to move, to enrapture, to seduce, to amuse and to depress. So it is very important that literature never falls into the wrong hands. It's worth bearing in mind that not all books are literature, in fact, some books are downright rubbish and were written specifically to waste paper.

Television: Recreating in the comfort of One's own home

Television isn't really what any One would call the highest of high culture, although it does occasionally have some quite interesting things on. The upper, upper classes or people of title watch a surprising amount of television, a trait they share with the peasantry. Whilst watching television is not necessarily un-Posh, *being* on telly is the most un-Posh thing in the world.

The next most popular way of recreating is perhaps ever so slightly tricky, in that it requires a very special sort of person to do it...

The Third Pillar: Sportism (and understanding the sportistic)

Theoretically, or at least historically, the sportistic activities developed spirit, comradeship and, as the Romans put it, '*mens sana in corpore sano*' (healthy in body, healthy in mind).

But developing physical prowess, the constant solitary commitment to improving the corporeal self – the Me – creates an inescapable addiction to endorphin-fuelled Me love. And it's never a pretty sight when straightforward self-esteem suddenly becomes auto-lust.

When sportism worked as a *Posh* pursuit it was because the goal was a jolly good time with the like-minded on a balmy day and the fee was a jolly good tea in the pavilion. But now it's done for very, very large suitcases of money with international underarm-deodorant advertising campaigns at stake. This means that the sportistic are prone to take themselves very seriously indeed.

Of all the ways of recreating, sportistic activity is the one that must be most carefully watched and regarded, for fear it slide inexorably into a morass of self-achievement. And the best way of checking so ignoble a descent is to watch sport a lot. Or at least to watch sportists in all their club-tongued freakishness whenever they're not actually doing sportism but when they are talking about their sportistism.

They really are marvellous to behold, fish most frantically out of water trying desperately to use their over-developed muscles to speak. One really shouldn't mock the afflicted, but when the affliction in question is so assiduously self-inflicted, then it really is very hard indeed not to giggle.

There are many, many ways of indulging One's sportistic self using just One's own over-developed mutations, but there are also other implements designed for the purposes of sportism.

So should One sport with balls?

Chasing balls for pleasure and/or profit

CRICKET – still carries with it a faint whiff of suburban genticity. But, as an institution, it's fighting a losing battle against mega-bucks and the venal. However, so long as there's a slap-up tea involved and the sportists wear nicely cut long trousers, then there's hope.

FOOTBALL – is, apparently, a gentleman's game played by thugs, whereas RUGBY is a thug's game played by gentlemen. Irrelevant, really. The days of gentlemen automatically being Posh are well and truly over. Rugby is, one admits, less narcissistic than football, but then it would have to be. Facial injuries in rugby are, it seems, an important part of the game, and it's difficult truly to love a reflection that's bull-necked, toothless, boasting an empty left eye socket and with an almost entirely detached lower lip. Oh, and half an ear missing. But the most awful injury in rugby has to be the unbridled agony and embarrassment of scrum rash, caused when the

wet, salty abrasion of coarse inner thigh hair meets the unguarded face
of the sportist so very close behind. It's Mother Nature's way of cruelly
marking rugby sportists so they may be recognised and avoided in the
street (in the same way she uses blond highlights, plucked eyebrows and
spray-on tans to single out footballerists and their wives in public).

GOLF – boasts its good points loudly. Fresh air, lovely views, a nice walk,
but it fails *Poshness* spectacularly on two fundamental points:

1) Wardrobe – there's absolutely nothing one can say in defence of golf
clothes. They're neither decorative nor useful, and they spitefully draw
attention to the particularly unattractive looseness of the middle-aged
male torso.

2) Landscaping – wherever One is in the world, Barbados, Gleneagles,
Tokyo, Crawley or Dubai, the landscaping of golf courses speaks a
peculiar horticultural language of contorted conifers, cultivised rockeries
and quixotically manicured lawns. For a nation of gardeners, a nation
that bore Capability Brown, Gertrude Jekyll, William Kent and
Humphrey Repton, why is Britain's most significant horticultural export
a landscape derived, one can only assume, from the front garden of a late
1960s bungalow just outside Cheam? Neat as a pin but dull as fuck.

BASKETBALL – is played by sportists who are happy to reach things down
from a top shelf.

NETBALL – is the same as the above but played by bossy ladies wearing
initialled bibs over cleverly stowed chests of amplitude.

HOCKEY – is played by the same ladies in slightly longer skirts with shoes
more sensible than the job really requires.

BOWLS – fills in time before death.

SNOOKER – fills in time before life.

POLO – There's no escaping or denying it, polo is *Posh* incarnate.
Unfortunately, it's only for the rich. Everything about it is as elegant as
elegant can be, from the jodhpurs which flatter the tautened thigh to the
canvas-awned spectator seating arranged as for a medieval tournament.

It's the cat's pyjamas of *Poshness* and one of those situations (like being in Venice, walking through the revolving door at the Ritz or writing a cheque) impossible for One not to feel waves of *Posh* crash orgasmically over One.

Wet fun for every One

SAILING – is rarely a comfortable experience and, when undertaken competitively, all of the fun is washed overboard. Technically speaking, *Posh* sailing doesn't really require a vessel or water, since the main ingredients are a lovely view, a nice breeze, elegantly served alcohol and horizontal stripes, all of which may be enjoyed on *terra firma*.

WATER SPORTS – such as windsurfing, water-skiing and surfing, all carry with them a youthful, informal attitude that is engaging and attractive but never really *Posh*. They're the sort of sportism the young and the clean do before becoming properly *Posh* and, since all require a pitch of aesthetic perfection, they're not exactly sportism for all. Surfing beaches are soon to receive aesthetic checkpoints at which the ugly in suction-tight neoprene will be basely abused and refused entry to the spume.

SYNCHRONISED SWIMMING – requires some of the loveliest outfits imaginable to do sportistic pursuits in. The combination of flower-studded bathing hat and orthopaedic nose clip is quite *non pareil* in the fashion stakes. And, what's more, the long-term use of very specific exercises creates in synchronised swimmers an ability for a far wider akimbo than any other water-borne mammal.

Cold fun for every One

SKIING – still carries a whiff of glamour which is always belied by the scruffy reality of queues, passes, over-excited school trips and that unendurable pain one gets from having ski boots tightened. Never forget that ski-boot technology was actually pioneered by the Spanish Inquisition.

SKATING – is by its very nature of propalism so very, very elegant. It's the closest thing a human creature can get to the exquisite glide Queen Elizabeth I was so famous for. Unfortunately, skating rinks are bestial places full of those of a brutish disposition.

Animal fun for every One

RACING – All racing, regardless of the carbon-based life forms competing, can be *Posh*, provided it's done elegantly. Racing is, after all, the least complicated of sportisms: there's a start, a finish and a race between.

Killing things for fun

KILLING THINGS – for pleasure is a tricky one these days, since it's impossible not to upset some One or other. But, philosophically, there's nothing wrong with celebrating One's position at the top of the food chain by killing off lower life forms left, right and centre. Indeed, there's really nothing to beat a good old-fashioned beaver hunt. With the right sort of ritualistic elegance and a nice outfit, even killing One's own species for pleasure or profit shouldn't be ruled out – look at lacrosse, ice hockey and line dancing.

HUNTING THINGS – is different to killing things, in that the hunting doesn't always end up with the killing bit. Everybody looks fabulously smart, which is a good thing, and it's always amusing seeing crusty elderly men wearing pink just so they may hunt foxes. Solitary hunting carries with it a heavy and rather worrying dose of sociopathic lonerism to it. But then, let's face it, it is technically known as 'stalking'.

And let's not forget

DARTS – is a funny game. Since pubs outside cities are gloriously classless places where all mingle without rancour, it's a surprise darts is so fearfully down-market. Milkmen are very good at darts because they are so very good at adding up.

DOING KEEP FIT – isn't really a form of sportistic activity and should never, ever be done in public. It's a solitary vice which one conducts merely to remain true to one's tailoring.

The Fourth Pillar: Posh
entertaining and entertainment

Now One has to attempt to put One's self in an unimaginable position and try as hard as One might to imagine a world where One were allowed only one sort of recreation. Should this happen, the only possible option would be to cling to the buoyant wreckage of the last and the most mighty Posh way of recreating: the wondrousness of entertaining and being entertained.

Posh and sociability

Being Posh all on One's own with no One but One's self for company would be so very, very difficult, not to mention lonely. After all, the Posh really are born to share and be shared. The very act of being Posh, when all's said and done, is to be extremely sociable. The Posh swarm, flock or pack themselves into vast, gregarious, highly amused and amusing herds which then wander majestically across the landscape of society. From waterhole to waterhole, from summer pasture to winter grazing, the Posh perform an essential peripatetic ecological function. As any market gardener or social engineer will tell you, without the seasonal passage of handmade shoes over the Home Counties of southern Britain, Cape Cod, the Hamptons or Antibes, the 'right kind' of dust would not be so persuasively released into the atmosphere to make those lovely pink-skied sunsets the world so thoroughly enjoys. Not to mention the fact that the Posh look quite, quite marvellous as a mass of loveliness, moving as a One.

The social season

Since the Posh are so very compelled to congregate in one place at the same time, specific annual events have been invented and exquisitely designed to form a decorously social backdrop to the festivities. Some of these events have been rather hijacked by upper-class people, since their own social engagements are poor, dull things by comparison.

The social season traditionally starts in April and finishes in October, which presupposes One has something else to do for the rest of the year. Perhaps One has a job, or helps out with meals on wheels. But compressing everything into the nicest months is a real boon for the wardrobe, since One needn't worry too much about having to keep warm.

The highlights of the Social Season:

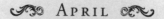

APRIL

The start of the polo season

The Oxford v. Cambridge boat race

The Christian Lacroix Gold Medallion handicap for rather
long-in-the-tooth fillies

The Chelsea Art Fair

The Belgravia Loveliness Fair

Queen Latifa's All-Comers Flower and Bulb Festival

The Taipei Open Cast Mining Corp. Embroidery Championships

MAY

The Royal Caledonian Ball

The Princess Derek of Luxembourg Memorial
Knightsbridge Shopathon

The Royal Windsor Horse Show

The Royal Small Rodent and Caged Duchesses Championships

The Chelsea Flower Show

The beginning of the Glyndebourne Festival opera season

The America's Cup

The Surrey Annual (what's the) Point to (what's the) Point

✥ JUNE ✥

The Royal Academy Summer Exhibition

The Epsom Derby

The Derby Epsom Salts Gargling Championships

The Royal Highland Show

Trooping the Colour

Flaying the Flag

Glastonbury Festival of Mud and Lager

The Queen's Cup Polo Final

Opening of HMP Holloway Open to All-Comers Madrigal Season

The Grosvenor House Grab a Granny and Knobbly Knees Festival

Opening of the Henley Royal Regatta

Royal Ascot

The Duke of Earl Stakes at Epcot

National Photocopier Day

National Wear One's Shirt with Pride Day

The International Day of Rusk and Hard Biscuit Tolerance

❧ JULY ❧

Glorious Goodwood

Inglorious Godalming

Injurious Ipswich

The Royal Show

The Buxton Opera Music and Brass-Rubbing Festival

Hampton Court Palace Flower Show

Opening of the Henry Wood Promenade Concerts

The Skittle Season begins

Snog a Scot Day (only if the 18th falls on a Tuesday)

The CLA Game Fair

The PG Tips Fair Play Game Fair

The Tin Pot Cup Open Polo Championships

Cowes Week

Sheep Month

Decade of the Pig Begins

ᴀ~᠅᠑ AUGUST ᠑᠅᠅

Edinburgh Military Tattoo

Edinburgh Minge Festival

Galloway Pony Trail Festival

Inverness Naval Tattoo and Piercing Day

Dublin Horse Show

Ballater Highland Games

Edinburgh International Festival

Glasgow and Region Hobby and Stitches Fair

Festival of British Embalming

Shooting Things in Earnest Day

❧ SEPTEMBER ❧

St Leger Festival

St Bernard Festival Booze-carrying Dog Championships

The Chatsworth Country Fair

Bracewear Royal Highland Gathering

The Last Night of the Proms

The Last Night of the Central Heating not being on

Chelsea Antiques Fair

The Westminster International Apple Pie Your Bed Event

Wear a Large Hat Day

National Celebrate the Children Going back to School Day

International Gay Speed Dating Championships

❧ OCTOBER ❧

The Beginning of Muff Month

Prix de l'Arc de Triomphe

Wexford Festival Opera

Opening of the Peasant-Buffing Season

National Swishing through large piles of Fallen Leaves Championships

Princess Jeremy of Elsenor Memorial Frog-Wearing Trophy

It is quite obvious, the social season revolves around all four of the Posh ways of recreating – shopping, culturism, sportism and entertaining. It gives those genuinely interested in this fascinating collection of shiny, perfectly dressed people an opportunity to study the Posh at first hand. Perhaps even from an open-topped Land Rover.

The anti-social season

Rather inevitably, the un-Posh saw quite how much fun the Posh were having and decided that they too should have a season during which they could all get together and smell strongly of cooked onion.

It starts on St Harrumph's day, late in August, with the first ball kicked in footballeristic anger and the now traditional lager vomiting festival at Hay on Wye. It then continues through the cold, wet months of winter, during which far too few clothes will be worn by its participants, until grinding to a halt with a huge National Poll Tax riot in April. It's all best avoided really.

Having a Posh evening

Above and beyond the organised activities and contrived splendorousness of the season, One can of course make One's own social entertainment. This is a lovely way of really making an evening come alive, and it creates a fabulous excuse or two to wear something jaw-dropping and improbably lovely from some clever fashion designer or other.

In addition to the requisite solids to eat and lovely things to drink, which are covered in the next chapter, having a Posh evening requires One to perform a series of tasks to guarantee its success.

1) Invite people. One of the very secrets of success about having a Posh evening is to ask people to come and share it with One. Any ordinary people would do but, actually, it's far better to ask Posh people, since they're guaranteed to provide charming conversation and somewhere really lovely to put One's eyes during the evening. They may well bring a lovely present, too.

2) Wear something nice and do a lovely 'do' with One's hair.

3) Lay on some marvellous, diverting entertainment. Magicians who steal One's watch, then hammer it into a million pieces through a silk handkerchief are always fun. As are sword-swallowers. But other people organise some One to come and sell items of intimate kitchen equipment or, better still, items of intimate feminine enrapturement which are driven by batteries. It's important, if such a party is planned, that One's guests understand they are not required to bring their own.

4) Set a room aside for people's coats and umbrellas.

5) Have some absolutely wonderful flowers with some truly inspired and rather unusual combinations, such as rusty barbed wire with ornamental brassicas or a Macintosh bow with Oxeye daisies.

Attending a Posh evening

Attending a Posh evening which One has been asked to attend has a few additional responsibilities attached to it.

1) On the morning of the evening, have flowers delivered. It shows such consummate, fabulous forethought. It's one thing to send flowers *after the event* but *before* means the generous host or hostess of the evening has one less arrangement to consider.

2) Look about as close to perfection as possible.

3) Be about as close to perfection as possible.

4) Be punctual. Arrive exactly fifteen minutes after the time One was invited.

5) Drink neither too little nor too much. The onus is quite squarely on the shoulders of the guest to show appreciation by being as ornamental as possible.

6) Sing for One's supper. Should One have a specific talent for anything such as singing or playing an instrument, then it would be a very thoughtful gesture to use that ability to entrance the other guests. Ladies who have undergone particular training in the Oriental ways of Pat Pong ping pong and gentlemen with overlarge or unusually shaped finery should start the ball rolling.

Clubbing

As a way of passing a Posh evening with friends, clubbing has rather fallen out of favour, due to the general decline in the number of seals.

Nightclubbing

Small, subterranean box rooms in the fashionable (or soon to be fashionable) districts of towns or cities are often used as nightclubs. Nightclubs always feel very, very naughty indeed, and those who go to nightclubs quickly develop a reputation for fast behaviour and loving and leaving. One can always spot nightclub attendees, thanks to their sleep-deprived, red eyes and bogies with an unusually high glitter content.

Nightclubs are places to enjoy should One really and truly not care about money. They are extravagantly and masochistically expensive. In return, apart from a very naughty evening indeed, nightclubs have special lighting to make One look the best One possibly could look. Unless, of course, One is silly enough to dance, in which case all One's loveliness is quickly borne southwards on a veritable torrent of sweat and ultra-violet light. Which does indeed rather neatly lead One on to the fraught question of dancing. Should One or shouldn't One?

Posh dancing

Unfortunately, Posh dances don't happen that often (except on television). Posh dances offer ways of dancing without fear of publicly sweating, disturbing One's shoulder line or compromising One's hairdo.

In Scottsland, there are ways of dancing which they themselves refer to as 'reeling', which have been designed not to be inelegant. They are, however, extraordinarily complicated. It must be said that the point of Scottish reels is rather lost if One doesn't actually wear the outfits to match.

Waltzing was (and still is in soon-to-be-dead circles) a lovely way of dancing. It was considered elegant and rather sexy if One's tastes were quite frigid.

The Tango hasn't ever really taken off in the way everyone expected it to, which is a real shame. It's a lovely, mannered way of beating up One's wife and should really be more widely explored. Tango's reputation has been much dented by the fact that all drunk people think they can do it.

Salsa dancing is growing in popularity. It requires a little too much flexibility of groin and wiggling of finery for gentlemen to feel entirely at home with it, but it remains the dance of choice for ladies who've gone dancing with their homosexualist best friend.

Line dancing encourages comradeship and team spirit, whilst the motions themselves have a certain 'bubble-gum hip' to them. Shame, then, that line dancing in all its forms is quite so bonnet-punishingly common. As for the inflammable outfits, self-harm hair and odeur de pasty which all go to make a jolly good evening line dancing, well …

So, when recreating from home (or indeed from homes) becomes either samey or dull, there's always the thought of recreating somewhere else. It's a lovely idea to broaden One's horizons occasionally, and the *Posh* are more than unusually adept at taking their lovely, sociable selves and their gorgeous ways of Genticity all over the world.

One's vacation

The *Posh* way is not to see One's daily life as a kind of chore-ridden drudgathon from which One needs periodic escape. The idea really is to engorge One's life to the extent that work and play blur and merge. With this in mind, *Posh* holidays come with none of the compulsive hysteria ordinary people attach to the idea of leaving One's life behind. Indeed, the *Posh* take their lives with them but just do them in different time zones. *Posh* holidays are gentle, relaxed, wafty things, where days extend in a bliss of subtle, elegant experiences. *Posh* holidays have no space for binge-drinking. Twenty-four-hour drinking should not, however, be discouraged.

Hotels: Paying for it by the night

The secret with hotels is to find one that feels very much like One really ought to live there. Some hotels are excessively modernistic, which leads One to suspect an out of body experience whenever One goes to the loo during the night. Turning on taps can sometimes be a quiz in itself, as can deciding which back-lit, shiny, white trough is the basin and which is the loo.

Other hotels are conceived to be exactly like staying with an extremely upper-class relative. Sometimes, extremely upper-class people are laid on as part of the service. Sadly, sometimes they are not.

The best sort of hotels are the hotels that have been hotels for really rather a long time. They've got it right, got used to it and every One employed there knows how to make the experience work. They're not necessarily very nice to One, but then who on earth needs to be vindicated by other people's niceness? The hotels themselves don't look fashionable or interestingly modernistic but, by and large, they tend to have absolutely marvellous views of where they are, because that's why they're there in the first place.

Proper packing

There is always a violent compulsion to pack absolutely everything, including the kitchen sink, which is ridiculous. After all, it's inconceivable that One's destination won't have a kitchen sink, so don't lose valuable space by packing it. Do, however, pack absolutely everything else. It is extraordinary how some people survive for months on the contents of one back-pack. But then, they're very often poorly dressed under-groomers who frankly should spend as much time as possible in dirty, remote places, where they're bound to fit in. As a general rule, allow four large stout pieces of luggage per person, per week. However, this may prove inadequate if a period of national mourning is announced.

As far as household necessities are concerned, it's essential to travel with the right kind of candelabra to tide One over, but candles are available more or less everywhere these days, so they can be purchased locally (unless, of course, One requires a particular colour. Mauves are very tricky to find on the Pacific Rim).

Turn One's jackets and coats inside out and fold them between sheets of tissue paper to keep them fresh-looking and uncreased. The colour of the tissue paper is irrelevant, although vigarious patterns must be avoided. A discreet polka dot or formal stripe will make sure your packing feels loved.

Lace-up shoes may be strung together and worn as a necklace if space is limited in One's trunk. Always pack under-garments alphabetically.

Travelling in style like a tasteful tortoise

It is important to stamp One's lovely personality on every space One inhabits, be it a train carriage, aeroplane seat or bobsleigh. To help, here is the absolute basic checklist of civilised travelling necessities:

* A stout silken rope and four brass stands to rope off One's personal travelling space
* An eighteenth-century porcelain incense burner and spearmint incense cones to ward off malevolent smells from fellow travellers
* The complete works of Dickens (leather-bound and hollowed out to conceal the things required to stock a decently appointed drinks tray)
* A Gentleman's Gentleman with a bit of Sherpa in them
* Earth of One's home country in a decorative box
* A huge amount of luggage
* Marmite

Cabin Staff — a breed apart

At this point, it is essential to digress momentarily to discuss the necessary evil that is the flight attendant. Orange from birth and cursed with fifteen more teeth than any other species, the lineage of the flight attendant can be traced back to the early nineteenth century, when a travelling dry-cleaning-fluid salesman married an orang-utan called Marjory. The resulting progeny, mutated and unmannered as it was, lived in hiding until somebody invented the aeroplane and it was discovered that the particular genetic foibles that set this new breed apart were in fact ideal for the newly created role of cabin crew. So, to improve the travelling experience, consult the following checklist:

* Try to avoid blinking and keep the gaze of the flight attendants in a tight mindlock. Meanwhile, intone in a low growl the ancient mantra, 'Upgrademe, upgrademe, upgrademe, upgrademe'
* Keep the vocabulary limited, pronunciation firmly sibilant and hand gestures expressive if One requires anything from a flight attendant
* Avoid at all costs being black-balled from the Mile High Club
* Above all, remember to augment One's air rage with a smile; it's so much more efficient

Remember, for all their vacu-smiles and banalarisms, they are there to help. Most importantly of all, they know glamour when they see it. They see Posh and all the loveliness Posh stands for as a concept to be much respected. They are also highly skilled at being covertly bitchy towards the rude, smelly and unpleasant. Really, One can learn a thing or two from them.

Travelling in, on, under and over things

EXTREMELY LARGE SHIPS were once very comfortable and luxurious and were a joy in which to travel. Now, they have sixteen-storey-high, shiny atriums and generally resemble floating shopping centres.

TRAINS are nothing like as romantic as they used to be, the lighting is harsh, and train travellers, by and large, stare a lot. Some, quite shamelessly, mentally undress One.

HOT AIR BALLOONS lack space for luggage but are terribly 𝒫osh.

MOTOR CAR journeys are obviously convenient and allow the possibility of in-car-styling to ensure the vehicle feels comfortable and fits One's own aesthetic. Cars don't work underwater, which really must be understood if One fancies popping to Europe.

FERRIES were created so One may pop to Europe. They have space for One's motor car, which may be taken on trips like a family pet. Ferries have restaurants where One may eat all One can eat. This produces vomit in more than insignificant quantities, the smell of which, after a long ferry journey, is impossible to remove from the softly upholstered parts of One's motor car. Most annoying.

AEROPLANES are gaining in popularity (with no thanks to Budget Air-Rage), although it is important to remember that, when stepping on to an aeroplane, One should never turn right. An acquaintance of our pot pourri-encrusted Authors once did indeed turn right and found behind a heavy curtain an acreage of surprised-looking people in tiny, miniaturised seats.

Recreation Myths

As One's ability to recreate becomes so unutterably compromised by the meagre space allowed in One's busy life to recreate in, the act of recreating becomes so much more important. Right recreating is a gift from the Gods. It's a celebration of the civilised and a simply super way of getting out from underneath the staff's feet.

CHAPTER SEVEN

One's Digestion

Digesting: The inescapable truth

There are those who say both noisily and aggressively that digestion is wholly natural and something to be celebrated, indulged and, worse still, shared with all. To begin, inserting the stuff to be digested has long been a sociable experience with a rich history of genticity and civility. The reverse is true of what happens at the other end. There are no traditions of sociability or exquisitely mannered ballets of etiquette. No, at the climax of One's relationship with One's meal, One is very, very much on One's own. Digestion really is a game of two ends, and the reason is perfectly simple: it is absolutely impossible to void the contents of One's digestive tract with anything even remotely approaching elegance.

Why It's So Very Important that Digesting is Done Poshly

Digesting, like copulating, is one of the baser primal urges. Everything in the world does it; even plants soak sunlight up through their greedy, green leaves so they may photosynthesise themselves rotten. In fact, it was probably seeing wild dogs eating old bits of elk whilst simultaneously adopting a tense squat so they may curl one out that inspired early man to invent civilisation in the first place.

Civilisation is the thing One treats One's self to when One develops an interest beyond recognising One's own species by close-contact sniffing. What was once a snarling pack of aggressive humanoids loosely banded together by a shared interest in each other's alimentary canals evolved into a mutually supportive, pacific society of happy homo erecti. And enshrined and celebrated at the centre of so brave a new world are the key concepts of sharing and mutual respect, which are, of course, the two basic, raw ingredients of table manners.

Now, at the heart of *not* celebrating One's digestive processes is the laudable desire to work hard to marginalise all that's animalistic in life. It gives One a daily, even hourly, opportunity to enjoy the fruits of evolution which create in One an ability to master the appetites and passions to which all lower life forms are but slaves. If a prairie dog feels a pang of hunger, it will immediately rectify the situation. But when any One civilised feels the same pang, an elegantly efficient system of self-control perfected over thousands of years is activated, producing patience enough to wait for a table to become free at the Ivy. And, of course, mankind has long moved away from the need to urinate on the move, like wild dogs. Apart from the French, that is.

Eating: The Good, the Bad and the Terribly, Terribly Ugly

Ugly eaters are people with little or no self-control and minimal self-esteem. They have an innate immaturity which refutes the importance of self-restraint or consideration for others. Ugly eaters are only too often also under-groomers, and they will almost certainly die friendless in slovenly poverty.

The five Tribes of ugly eaters are:

* At number five, WOLFERS wish so very dearly that natural selection would eventually provide them with a wide, fleshy lower jaw like a threadbare satchel which could be used to scoop food up and then propel it (following a messy, airborne triple salchow) straight into a foaming gullet. They'll often hide behind the excuse that they 'enjoy their food'. In fact, they're really just greedy and selfish. Never, ever wait for a Wolfer to share anything and, should One find One's self next to a Wolfer at table, wear something cunningly tailored from something shiny and moisture-repellent like a good old-fashioned macintosh.

* Number four plays host to FUSS-POTS, whose selfishness manifests itself in an all-too-attention-grabbing show of fuss and bother about what they can or can't eat or what they do and don't like. (As if any One cared.) Of course, there are those who genuinely do have problems digesting certain foodstuffs but, generally speaking, they're the plucky Ones who eat green peppers or peanuts or wheat or whatever it is their badly made stomach can't digest and then swell or choke in private so as not to cause commotion. Fuss-pots should almost certainly be deprived of food and most definitely deprived of *all* attention.

* CAR-EATERS are at number three. These are sullen, secretive people who are unable to control their animal appetite and who feel compelled, like the lower life form they are, to seek out a dark private place in which hastily to devour their scavenged prize. Their clothes are perpetually speckled with mayonnaise and pebble-dashed with pasty crumbs. The exhaust pipes of Car-eaters' cars should really be stuffed full of bananas so that their cars fill quickly with carbon monoxide. That'll put them off their food soon enough.

* The penultimate food crime comes from CUD-CHEWERS. Cud-chewers are misguided into thinking that their way of eating has a delicacy and Genticity to it. They'll chew and chew and chew and use their cutlery like crochet hooks. All pickety, pickety, pickety. Eating a meal with a Cud-chewer takes for ever, but not in a marvellous, rambling, Mediterranean way but in a painfully, meagrely, mealy-mouthed way. Cud-chewers often have barely repressed Freudian issues which give them guilty pleasure when either end of the alimentary canal is fiddled with. A traditional treatment for the Cud-chewer is to nail their hands to the table either side of their plate and make them eat hot pork fat.

* But the worst and ugliest way of eating is STREET-EATING. There is not a single human appetite or urge that should be satisfied whilst walking down the street. One doesn't pop to the bank whilst unashamedly self-polluting, One doesn't defecate on the hoof and no One returns from a trip to the supermarket laden with carrier bags and spontaneously and cheerfully urinating as they go (apart from, of course, the French). No, so why should the messy consumption of lard-oozing burgers, malodorously flaccid, hot sausage rolls and malevolent pasties be somehow sanctionable? For Street-eaters, the most earth-shatteringly important, compelling and urgent issue is their own hunger. Not that the oil-seeping, shuffling dollops of moribund adipose can really be that hungry, since it must have been

all of minutes since they last self-administered their previous dose of animal-fat-flavoured carbohydrate. What they have is a deeply unhealthy if not morbid obsession with ensuring that their cake-hole is perpetually filled often with cake. Street-eaters should be treated for what they are, a mutated subspecies of regressed humanoid that look revolting and make a mess wherever they go.

Anti-social eating: Food fads

One of the principal problems with people is that they're always looking around for some One else to blame for anything they don't like about themselves. There are those who have decided that all that's wrong in their life is caused by their attitude to food. These people like things to believe in, and for them there are books with medical-sounding titles which give them all sorts of contradictory advice. But, really, the only thing that's true about food that nobody seems to have noticed and that your chopstick-literate Authors are going to reveal to you now is that *too little makes One thin and too much makes One fat.*

Diets

As any One who knows some One who is doing dieting will tell you, those who do diets are the most frightful bores. Really, One is faced with a choice if One feels One has reached a degree of unacceptable tubbtitude. Either redesign everything about One's self as befits One of amplitudeousness or shut up about it.

Eating: A how-to

Eating properly has much in common with the bluff business of engineering. What gets raised up to and then inserted into the mouth should not, obviously, exceed the mouth's capacity to contain it. And, remember, it's not just to be contained by the mouth but it has to be moved from one side to another so it may be chewed.

The process of raising food to face should be undertaken with equipment suitable for the consistency of the food. The food in question should not be made into pieces so small it encourages pernickety cud-chewing. One's lips must always be closed over the teeth during chewing (if nothing else, a simple safety precaution). Effort not to make excessive noise during the process will be aided by closed lips, as will the avoidance of spillage or splattering. A kindness to all.

One may speak with One's mouth full, provided what One's mouth is filled with is discreet enough not to be inelegantly on show as One speaks and One doesn't embark on a lengthy conversation. And One must make what One says interesting enough to be worth it. But, when all's said and done, the eyebrow is an immensely eloquent ally at the table, allowing for a broad range of replies as well as a limited number of questions without disturbing One's ability to continue chewing. Do, however, avoid packing so much food into One's cheeks that One resembles a foraging chipmunk or, indeed, the late Marlon Brando dressed as a foraging chipmunk.

The secret of successful food consumption is to avoid the excesses of over-enthusiasm and/or prissiness. Show hearty enjoyment by all means and strive to maintain an elegance of manner and movement but, remember: 'sharing' and 'mutual respect' in all things. The more dandified grandees of the Spanish Inquisition created a special place in hell for sinners with bad table manners. In this dark and sulphurous Hades of perpetual torment, those who eat ill will be continuously punished by having their unguarded genitals cruelly placed on a heated hostess trolley until they be cooked.

Table manners: The charmoury

The word 'sharing' and the term 'mutual respect' should really be tattooed on the breast of all those who sit down at a table to eat. They are the Alpha and the Omega of table manners. In between there's a whole alphabet of rules and regulations, a veritable table-top highway code designed to make the eating experience as civilised as possible. As with all rules, they can be bent (elegantly), they may be broken (stylishly) but, none the less, One needs to know them or else there'll be a horrific pile-up at the bread basket or a jam traffic jam at the jam.

1) **Know your zone** – at the dining table, every One is given an allotted space carved fairly from the whole. To exceed One's space means an intrusion into some One else's space, which (even if One's invited) is wrong. This rule serves a very practical purpose really. It ensures that One doesn't reach out for something and knock the food from a neighbour's fork or trail One's pendent brocade cuff in another's ganache. The calculation of a personal exclusion zone is the extent to which One can reach whilst keeping One's elbows neatly folded into

One's sides. Plus, by keeping to this rule, One also ensures that One is prepared just in case another One's filthy thieving fork makes an attack on One's own private plate.

2) **Traffic flow** – always pass to the left. Vegetables, bread, wine, water or herbal cigarettes, it doesn't matter, always to the left. Likewise, in restaurants or at a dinner served by footmen, expect food to be in-coming over One's right shoulder and out-going from One's left. In certain circles, however, expecting footmen in-coming over One's right shoulder has an entirely separate complexion to it.

3) **Order of service** – always wait to start until invited by whoever has cooked or paid for the meal. But, should you be urged to start, then not to start is a terrible rudeness.

4) **Help One's self** – if offered a plate or dish of scrumptiously enticing edible objects, always obey the 'know your zone' rule and help yourself to the nearest within reach. In other words, no matter how tempting the biggest slice may be, there is no excuse for dragging One's cuffs across the platter to grab that fat prize at the opposite end.

5) **Tortoise and Hare** – try hard to finish neither first nor last, and always, always compliment everything. Should One find One's self defeated by the horribility of the food served, then make a fuss of accepting the blame: 'I'm stupidly full,' 'I was born with only half a tongue,' 'the valve on my colostomy bag needs renewing and, since you've just had these dining chairs re-upholstered, I daren't risk it. Sorry! – *Mea culpa!'* And, should the food be lovely, never ask for any more until *all* have finished eating.

6) **The Piece of Shame** – the very last solitary serving or portion left by all. The dilemma is all too obvious: if One pounces on it, One appears greedy; if One denies it, One seems uncomplimentary. The worst thing in the world is to subdivide it like a fussy spinster. No, robust Posh manners encourage the enjoyment of the piece of shame with a clear conscience. Greed be hanged.

Table manners: The armoury

As discussed, the choreography of decent digestion has become one of the expressions of civilisation which is most reverentially celebrated. The implements One uses to eat with have become an enduring symbol of the elevation mankind has engineered for itself away from the bestial hand-eaters we all once were. Cutlery is a real and metaphorical expression of the elegance we're capable of creating for ourselves.

As such, respect it. Don't play with it, use it flippantly, beat out the rhythm of a drum or pick One's nails with it. Don't hold it like a pen, a dart or a Viennesey little hand bell designed for summoning simpering catamites. Don't point with it, gesture with it or scrape it clean against the plate or a finger. When eating, the prongs of a fork should be kept facing down for as long as possible (or until One's compulsive greed for peas in quantity overrides the over-delicacy of spearing slippery little green spheres one by one).

If just a spoon and fork are laid, the spoon should be treated as an honorary knife, with all the eating done off the fork (old etiquette advocated the opposite, but it was wrong). However, cheese and peeled fruit may be eaten off the knife – but elegantly, elegantly only and always elegantly and, for One's own sake, just a little carefully.

Thanks to the late 1970s sitcom and specialist satellite stations (the Dinner Party Channel is a riot, by the way), there are few who do not know the sequence with which One uses the bountiful array of cutlery at One's place setting. If in doubt, just follow this one rule: start from the outside and always work One's way in. Keep an eye on an elder or senior guest to see how specialist equipment is to be used (unless they're so old their specialist equipment is a straw) and always follow the lead of the happy charming human whose invitation to dine One originally accepted.

As a refresher, please study the following menu and reconcile it with the diagrammatic place setting that follows:

* A clear soup (beware the fingerbowl) with breadity
* Shell-on shrimp and escargot salad
* Lamb served with broccoli, potatoes Dauphinoises and asparagus
* A light sorbet of gin and nicotine
* Angels on horseback
* Cheese
* Coffee and petits fours
* Prostitutes

If the hostess is a Duchess, the Femidom is placed beneath the napkin. Also don't forget all drinking vessels to the east should be filled with gin.

Confused? Don't be, practice does so make perfect.

Asparagus: A rule unto itself

One can buy asparagus dishes, which are longish, flattish and vaguely rectangular, and One can buy longish, flattish, vaguely rectangular tongs for serving asparagus, but search as One might, there's no such thing as an asparagus fork. That is because, for some unknown reason, One is allowed to hold the asparagus stalk at its widest point with One's own personal fingers, grasping the sap-rigid base of the shaft as One allows the moist and shiny swelling of the bulbous tip to caress the inside of One's parted lips. And after One's swallowed, all that's left is to lick the hot buttery overspill off One's salty fingertips. Marvellous and very confusing for foreign people.

Sauces for courses and condimentia

Just after God invented contagious diseases, he invented the butter knife. On most tables, there are items to be shared – butter, gravy, sauce, or what are commonly called 'condiments'. Serving One's self a nice big fat dollop of any of the above should very obviously not be done with any item of One's own personal cutlery that has more than likely been in One's own personal mouth. Butter is a fabulous example. A nice mellow pat of butter should be removed from the butter dish and placed on One's side plate using the butter knife, which One then replaces. The act of spreading butter should then be completed using One's smallest knife, wrought purposely for this purpose. This system, so fantastically civilised as it is, reduces the risk of ingesting another's toast crumbs, effluvia, stray pubic hairs or toenail clippings.

Napkin-Folding: One's way to success

There can be no shadow of a doubt: if Queen Marie Antoinette had been better at napkin-folding, the French Revolution would never have happened. It's a source of constant amazement that people today are put off this noble and historic art form, particularly since many continue to moan about not having enough creative outlets in their empty, echoing, irrelevant lives.

For those distracted by what's wrongly perceived as fuss and bother, study the following 'folds' (as they're known to purists), which have been specifically and most glamorously created by our porcelain-complexioned Authors:

The Portland Vase

The Macgregor

Hopefulness

The Jolly Golly Gash

The Lovers Knot

Mice in the Ballroom

The Poke Bonnet

The Poke in the Moonlit Churchyard

Seaman on the Poop

What is Posh Food, and Indeed What is Not?

Posh Food	Not Posh Food
Apples	Apple pie served in a greaseproof envelope
A bacon sandwich with tomato ketchup	A bacon sandwich without tomato ketchup
Lamb chops	Mutton chops (particularly on elderly peers)
Oysters on ice	Peas and rice
Peacock	Squirrel
Swan (roast)	Pineapple rings in syrup
Most pasta	Most pasties
Chilli chocolate lobster	Anything 'with all the trimmings'
Char-grilled vegetables	Anything with a hair in it
Cowboy pie	Anything with a thumb in it
Rare roast beef	Anything lapped out of a navel
Rare or endangered species	Rotten milk in all its forms
Balsamic vinegar	Bubble gum
A fish supper with a loved One	Snacks
Silver-service buffet	All you can eat for a fiver

Posh Party Food in all its Lovely, Celebratory Incarnations

Sharing One's Poshness with others is a joyful duty. One should relish with satisfied abandon any opportunity to throw open One's life, make it look even lovelier than usual, organise some most delicious food and contrive veritable gurgling cascades of lovely things to drink, all for the pleasure of people One knows. Or, indeed, those they don't yet know, since entertaining is a marvellous way of meeting new Ones.

There are several ways of entertaining One's friends, here are a few:

THE DINNER PARTY gives One a sensational opportunity to display One's aptitude at the Posh arts of table-laying, napkin- folding, flower-arranging, social placement, conversation, mingling and, in certain circumstances, lap dancing. Dinner-party food should be plentiful in its exquisity, with lots and lots of lovely little 'pickety' things One can feast on in a relaxed, conversational way. Take time to plan surprises; swans will always make guests gasp, but be sure to find a swan that has died from natural causes or else the Queen of Britain (who owns all swans) might get cross – even so far as to orchestrate the removal of One's head.

A BUFFET presents a blank canvas for the creative host or hostess. Buffets should be seen as a marvellous, marvellous still life which One may eat. Study the scrumptious compositions of the seventeenth-century Dutch masters and see how their rich, rippling effects may be interpreted using cheese cubes and pineapple squares on cocktail sticks. Please ensure there's always a heavy swag of some rich velvet or other. And a skull as a piquant *memento mori.*

Pot-Luck Parties, where all the guests bring something they've prepared but leave before washing up are fine if One is able to guarantee the quality of One's guests. And a nice way of inheriting any crystal bowls which are left behind.

Wife-Swapping Parties are rarely about the food, which makes sense, since it's all so very exciting One simply can't waste time eating.

Lynching Parties should revolve around a pretty decent spread of canapés themed to coordinate with the evening. Finger-borne food always works much better than a more formal sit-down meal with cutlery, for obvious reasons.

Barbecues are very rarely *Posh*. The food tends to be less than inedible, One's clothes become quickly wreathed in the acrid smell of impregnated coal, the white wine warm and the red wine sour and each decanted from a box. The plates are paper, the cutlery plastic and the conversation Australian.

Picnics, on the other hand, are, with a little effort, guaranteed to be *Posh*. The food should, as with a buffet, make a strong aesthetic statement in its own right and should be presented on a bevy of fine china dishes placed on stands in order that a pleasing variety of heights is achieved. As much formal dining furniture as may be carried by the household staff should be disposed around the area of picnicking. Be sure to pack One's wind-up gramophone.

Drinks Parties are slightly misleading in that they're not just about drinking. Eating things should be provided as well, although deep-fried and salt-coated carbohydrate in amusing shapes and various shades of brick dust should really be avoided. No, for a decent drinks party, One needs to embrace the potentially tricky issue of ...

The canapé: Sticks and stones may break my teeth

Canapés are marvellous, decorative little things which may be arranged in exotic patterns or served on unusual and diverting surfaces such as antique paving slabs, panes of mirror glass or bigger sea shells.

Canapés, thanks to their delicate size, should never be seen as a meal replacement, although there's talk of making them a food group in their own right. They should never be wolfed hungrily down nor, indeed, inhaled. The point of canapés is to create sophisticated and unusually flavourful combinations of tastes, colours and textures which delight most of One's nerve endings from the navel up.

But, since they are so very, very precious, canapés come with some serious points of order which must be observed:

* They should be more or less exactly one bite big. Anything likely to ooze, dribble or seep when bitten in half is disrespectful to the guest.
* Larger canapés which require multiple biting are possible but they will require their own handle or some sort of device so they may be conveyed to the face.
* Two-part canapés designed to be dipped in some attendant sauce or relish should only ever be dipped once. Going back for a second bite with some en-sticked canapé running in garlands of saliva is very, very wrong.
* The emptied stick or skewer which formerly impaled a canapé should never, ever be put back on the canapé plate. Thoughtful hosts provide receptacles amongst the canapés for waste product, otherwise polite guests should hang on to canapé detritus until a bin is found.
* Stones, bones and pips should be tactfully and elegantly removed or swallowed. Spitting, whilst amusing, can seem disrespectful, although it's worth seeing what One's host or hostess does and then follow their lead.

Removing Accidental Food from Bits of the Body

To be frank, the effective combination of One's exquisite table manners and the clever forethought of One's indulgent host or hostess should mean that food spillage is not an issue. If, however, a fleck or so slips under the net, then shake like a wet dog to dislodge any dry besmirchment or dribble like a goon in the general direction of a moist embarrassment.

Removing accidental food from bits of the body of somebody else

The human is a suggestible creature and will find itself unintentionally mimicking the movements of any One standing opposite them. So, should, perhaps due to some energetic conversational pyrotechnics, One inadvertently propel food at some One, simply scratch, itch or caress the landing zone on One's self and wait for the other person to follow in mirror image. This all, of course, presupposes that the application of food to another has not been planned specifically as an early course in a banquet of seduction. The spluttered propulsion of a half-digested mouthful aimed directly at another is, in this instance, known as an *'amuse bouche'*. (Later on in the sex cycle, it is known as an 'amuse bush'.)

Booze

Do please feel free to call an alcoholic beverage 'booze'. It's a word with a lovely jovial feel to it and is almost impossible to say without One's mouth forming a kissy kind of grin. Obviously, there are things to drink which aren't actually alcoholic (Indian tonic water being one), but they tend to be drinks that were in fact invented for drinking in the same glass as alcohol (Indian tonic water being one again). But they tend to be little fun.

Posh drinks

* Gin
* Gin and tonic
* Gin and tonic and ice
* Gin and tonic and ice and
  a thin bit of fruit
* A pint of gin and tonic
* Tonic and gin
* Pink gin (with tonic)
* Pink gin (without tonic)
* Pale pink gin
* Gin and tonic (straight from
  the bottle)
* A Pimm (please note:
  never a *Pimm's*)
* Red wine and white wine
  and Prosecco
* Sloe gin
* Ginger gin
* Some whiskey
* Guinness
* Gin and tonic (in a different glass, as a nightcap)

More on gin

Gin is by its very nature Posh, although few know why. It used to be very
cheap indeed, which meant that more people drank gin than drank water.
When Indian tonic water was derived from the bark of the quinine tree, gin
and tonic became the Posh people's favourite cure for malaria.

Gin looks marvellous and is best served in a cut-crystal glass but, should
One be very, very thirsty, it can be served in a nice vase.

A word on Pimm

The next most popular drink for the lovely end of society is a Pimm, made from a thick syrupy alcohol invented by a Mr Pimm, which One drinks with fizzy lemonade or ginger ale (or, better still, Indian tonic water) and a vast garnish of shrubbery.

Other booze

All other booze is more or less self-explanatory, apart from Prosecco, which is much nicer than Champagne and has a rather fetching and rustic piece of twine that keeps the cork in the bottle.

How to look sober when One clearly isn't

Should One not feel at all the ticket but want every One else to think One capable of operating heavy machinery, then follow the following:

* Move slowly and deliberately
* Hang on to things as you walk around
* Stand next to people drunker than One
* Don't smile inanely
* Don't leave intimate extremities of One's person hanging out
* Sit down with One's legs and fingers crossed as much as possible
* If all else fails, pretend to be foreign

Restaurants: The fine art of digesting in public

Restaurants are ideal places to eat for those who have no household staff, lest they have to cook their own food, serve at their own table and wash their own dishes. Indeed, some restaurants have been comfortably and discreetly furnished to make dining out feel as much like dining at home as possible, such as the Ritz in London and the Tour D'Argent in Paris.

There are other restaurants which are known to be 'fast' and which ask for very little money for the food they make, which may explain why it mostly looks regurgitated.

How to turn a maître d' into a maître d'elight

A restaurant, like society itself, needs a leader. There are many, many people who do all sorts of useful and important jobs in restaurants, but the only One who's any One is the *maître d'* (which is French for 'Master of ...', which is nice and mysterious really).

*Maître d'*s go to special schools to learn to be off-hand, where all of them practise looking down their nose. Truly great *maître d'*s have perfected the art of aggressive page-turning, which they do to great effect and with a baroquely licked forefinger whenever they need to flick through their large, important reservations books to see whether they want One to dine in their restaurant.

*Maître d'*s aren't actually that difficult or complicated to use. One has to remember that they are simply there to ensure that people who aren't *Posh* cannot enter, which is fine and quite commendable. All One has to do is satisfy the *maître d'* of One's *Poshness*, which really shouldn't be difficult.

Should One find One's self breaking in a new *maître d'*, then start off with the old-fashioned art of tipping. But, rather than a discreet high-denomination banknote palmed lavishly from One to another, bribe instead with a huge fruit basket, succulent wriggly piglet or ornamental flowering shrub in a decorative planter. Make the donation as eye-catching as possible and create as much fuss imaginable, and you'll always get top table.

Basic waiter management

Waiters are sort of junior *maître d's* who, in fact, do all the work. They fetch and carry and scurry around bringing One's food to One. It is upon their slender Italianate shoulders that the responsibility of providing One with exactly the right food One wants falls, so waiters require very, very firm handling indeed.

As with *maître d's*, always ensure waiters smell power when they approach One. Look them commandingly in the eye and be clipped to the point of curtness with One's initial instructions. But then, and here's the secret, gradually warm to them. Don't offer anything that might be misconstrued as a conversation, but be punctilious with thanks and gracious with praise.

When summoning a waiter, don't under any circumstances snap One's fingers, clap or call out anything other than 'Excuse me'. The most efficient technique is to wait until their faces are pointed in One's direction and then lock eyes in a guided-missile stare, allow a wraith of a half-smile to contract the side of One's mouth, then emphatically propel one eyebrow upwards. They'll run straight to you like a hungry puppy to a lactating bitch.

The following table of useful eyebrow vocabulary has been specifically designed to slide unnoticed in the breast pocket of a dinner jacket or a bejewelled evening bag in order that it may be consulted in any restaurant One might find One's self in.

Eyebrow commands for breaking in waiters

Hold me till the
hurt stops

Please bring
our coats

The béchamel has
separated

What time does
your shift finish?

May I have
the bill please

My glass is empty

May I have a kiss
please?

Bring salad
dressing now

My companion
needs tucking in

Bring a hand-held
vacuum cleaner
immediately

My companion
has much interest
in exploring your
trousers further

My room number
is written on the
napkin. Come to
me at midnight
with that large red
pepper grinder
of yours

And then, when all's said, done, digested and settled up, always leave the largest of imaginable tips discreetly under a napkin.

Menu French and how to speak it

Even menus in British restaurants are written in menu French, so it's important to know how to get One's tongue around it.

Menu French	Translation
Dans une sauce	In a sauce
Avec son jus	Cooked in its own seepage
Aux chips	With chips
Enrobé du chef	The Chef's licked this one
Délicieux	Coated in whatever it fell in when dropped
En saison	In season
En pannier	In a basket
En jupe et blouson	In a lovely skirt and top
Aux légumes	With a medley of vegetables
Aux médaillons	With a medley of medals
Avec éclat	With gusto
Avec le chat	With disgusto
Un seul cornichon	Just one Cornetto
A son choix	Cooked to your liking
A mon choix	Cooked to your licking

And, finally, perhaps the single most trickysome issue to be dealt with in a restaurant ...

How to determine who's paying before One orders

It's a sordid reality, really, but one which must, regrettably, be faced: One's food has to be paid for. Would it were different, but unfortunately it's not.

Now, when One is asked out to dine by some One else, it's a more or less universally acknowledged implication that the askee pays for the asked. Thus, as the menu is placed in One's hands, remark to One's companion, 'How kind you are, how lovely it is, but Heavens, how dear everything seems to be. Are you sure? How generous you are!' Whatever happens, don't leave enough room for an answer or a response in between the exclamations and, with any luck, not only will they accept responsibility for the bill, they'll also be compelled to invite One to order what One will (even down to the gold-plated lobster cutlets cooked in jewel jam served on a four-poster bed of crushed pearls soaked in fine Armagnac and peacock foie gras).

A second tactic is to head for the loo at the precise moment that you sense the bill is coming. This may take some practice, since it involves a honed sense of intuition. Failing that, excuse One's self for the loo and then, out of eye-shot, request that the bill be sent over to your table. Enjoy One's own reflection and fuss with One's hair long enough to emerge lovely, and then act surprised when you find that the bill has been paid in your absence. Thus, you neither have to pay nor suffer the embarrassment of watching your partner perform advanced calculus to work out the gratuity.

So, having become lulled into a soft, cosy, warm world of false security dealing with the top of One's alimentary canal, the time is now upon One to come face to face with ...

Bodily Functions: Naming and Shaming

The basics: from the front comes wee, and from the back comes poo. Anything that may come out of the mouth is sick (if it's wet), or a burp (if it's not).

These events should never be done in front of others (although burping – provided it's not too lusty or with too obvious relish – may be excusable, provided there's a flurry of tender delicacy around the event and an exquisitely worded apology).

It's best really not to go into too much detail when seeking to be excused so that One might void One's waste. A simple, 'Please excuse me' is sufficient, perhaps followed by a matter-of-fact request, 'May I please use your loo' or, more discreetly, 'Where may I find the loo', which quite rightly suggests that One's going to void whether permission is granted or not. Always remember: the loo should always be referred to as 'the loo', even in very, very foreign countries indeed. Although the word 'toilet' is understood by all, it'll never pass the lips of the Posh even if it would obviate the need to mime the word 'loo' to bemused Columbian cocaine-pickers. Note for Americans: request a bathroom when and only when One is actually planning to take a bath.

Wind: A two-way street

Poo is a fact of life One can really get One's teeth into, but wind is so much more intangible. Even the term 'wind' doesn't help, since burps and farts are quite obviously not some gentle, blossomy breeze that's spent a pleasant summer afternoon caressing a flower-studded Home Counties hillside.

No, wind is a noxious gas. There is absolutely nothing to relish, enjoy or in any way be proud of. Just as a big, juicy burp is most definitely not a hearty congratulation on a meal, so too a fart cannot be seen as a resonant overture to a turd well passed.

Cubicle etiquette

Being on a loo is a very, very private thing and One has to see One's tenure of the loo as momentary. Others will be using it after One and some may very well have used it before. So, like all tenancies great and small, One's time in the loo comes with certain responsibilities:

KEEPING ONE'S SELF TO ONE'S SELF – Always ensure One is snugly locked in. If there is no lock or bolt, wedge the door shut with a foot, whistle loudly to warn oncomers, or emulate the bestial grunts and sighs of a bricklayer making a poo the size of a brick. This should prevent any One blundering in.

WIPE-OUT – Should there be no loo paper, look around for a curtain with some densely close-repeating pattern that might do.

TITANICALLY UNSINKABLE – If One makes a poo that, like a bad (spent) penny, won't go away when flushed, weigh it down by studding it with as much small change as One can find in One's pocket.

EAU DE TOILETTE – If One fouls the air, don't reach out for some CFC-smelling, apricot-scented euphemism of an air freshener. Instead, remember that gas may be burnt off. Smart hosts will always leave casually within reach of the loo a box of matches for exactly this purpose.

Finally, cover One's tracks: leave the cubicle exactly as One would be so very relieved to find it.

The pissoir conundrum: How can One not look?

The British are quite adamant that, without a formal introduction, it is quite out of the question to speak to, look at, or form an attachment to a stranger. This is a particularly tricksy issue when One is shoulder to shoulder with another at the porcelain. One has to force One's eyes to bore deep, laser-like holes into the discoloured grout straight ahead. But then a manly meaty flutter just within reach of One's peripheral vision as a vein-girt flaccidige of gentleman's sex-suet waves hello. And, wham, the naughty eyes are on it and back before One knows it, before One can control it – oh, the shame! The worst of it is that it's not as if One may then seek out a formal introduction, since One simply can't shake hands with One's hands so very full. What is One to do?

Try blinkers, they work for randy racehorses.

So, is it Alimentary, My Dear Watson?

The business of feeding is simultaneously so very public and so very private. There may seem a lot of fuss and bother attached to something so simple, but the art of civilisation requires practice and sacrifice before the gilded cap badge of genticity may be awarded. Besides, if One thinks the natural act of digestion requires a lot of thinking about to get it to a Posh polish, imagine what's required to make the equally natural act of reproduction suitably civilised …

CHAPTER EIGHT

One's Reproduction

Basic Reproduction: The basics

Any One who has tried reproduction at its least complicated, i.e., when a gentleman leaves seed behind in a warm puddle into which a passing lady may squat on a whim, knows it to be so very hollow and unsatisfying. Yes, the to-ing and fro-ing, sucking and blowing, the fighting and reconciling which go with modern reproduction is undoubtedly high maintenance, but worth it in the end. Provided, of course, that it is done Poshly.

The bits required

For satisfying reproduction, specialist equipment is required. Luckily, thanks to evolution, humankind comes with just such specialist equipment attached. How lovely it is and how much fun it is to use.

One's reproductive bits should never be taken for granted simply because they come free. One should groom One's reproductive organs thoroughly and often. Keep them warm, make them feel loved, and you'll get hours and hours of pleasure from them.

Doing Sex

Doing sex was invented to provide great downstairs intimacy between people who didn't have the right kind of vehicle for the school run but still wanted all the fun of the fair. Doing sex caught on quickly; in fact, it spread (quite literally) like wildfire and soon every One was up to it or, indeed, down to it. But nearly every One has a different way of doing sex.

Here's a quick rundown:

HETROSEXUALISTS do sex based on the creative principle of the plug and the socket. Should One want to reproduce One's self then doing sex as hetrosexualists do is well worth a try.

HOMOSEXUALISTS elicit their pleasure from the fact that both parties have plugs. They are like sparkling, rainbow-hued bubbles which fill the air with high spirits and levity but are very, very bad indeed at reading maps. Homosexualists, like the Posh, enshrine at the core of their belief system the sanctity of good grooming and perfectly polished small talk. There have been moves officially to 'twin' homosexuability and Poshness, particularly after the lavish television adaptation of *Brideshead Revisited* in the early 1980s. So far, this has come to nothing, as the paperwork was far more complicated than any One realised.

VAGITARIANS are ladies who don't eat meat (such practice is also known to its intimates as Lesbianage). They have perfected socket-on-socket fun (or 'double declutching'). By and large (and indeed they can sometimes be both), vagitarians are clever, earnest people who hold down thoughtful jobs. They favour large, sheet-steel jewellery as a badge of their ancient and mysterious rites. Vagitarians are exactly the sort with whom One would wish to be stuck in a lift, since they are calm and practical and do not burden One with incessant jokes.

TRANSVESTITISTS When society decided with such brutality not to allow gentlemen the basic human right to wear silky, lacy clothes, transvestitists came together and decided nonetheless to sport the only silky, lacy clothes they could get hold of, which, of course, meant shopping in ladies' boutiques.

EXHIBITIONISTS hang around in groups outside museums.

DOMINATRIXES are bossy women who are on top of every situation. The world is full of them.

TRANSEXUALISTS would rather be an entirely different gender altogether. They are easy to spot what with their large hands and polyester blouses.

These are just a few. There are many, many, many ways of doing sex, involving dressing up, dressing down, emissions, omissions, straps, flaps and scat but, at the end of the day, it requires a minimum of two carbon-based life forms. All, that is, except …

Oneanism: A solitary vice? Or finger-lickin' fun for every One?

Sometimes, the very Poshest of folk find themselves with an irresistible desire for themselves. In fact, thinking about it, it's something of a surprise that the Posh (who are so very, very lovely) ever leave themselves alone. Oneanism, or self-bothering, was, for most of the last 2,000 years, frowned upon as a waste of a gentleman's potentially useful seed. When executed by a lady, it was seen as an unnecessary distraction from needlework, or pressing flowers.

In today's far more tolerant society, self-pollution is tolerated as an acceptable activity when One's television set breaks down or when One has specific permission to 'work from home'.

Modern Mating:
Meeting a Mate to Mate with

Before sex may be done, One needs to find some One with whom to share One's fluids. Meeting a mate to mate with is a fascinating topic. One already knows that to be Posh is to be as glamorous and attractive on the inside as One is on the outside, but being glamorous and attractive on the outside means that One will indeed attract others in quantity. It's like walking on a windy beach with a thick layer of sticky lip-gloss. It is therefore of paramount importance that One only shows One's self to other creatures to whom One would wish One's self to be attractive. So where does One go to find friends to share in downstairs fun?

THE DINNER PARTY The dinner party provides an ideal shop-window to display One's wares in flattering candle-light, with plenty of lovely food and loads of wine to soften the focus. Little surprise then, that our own much marvelled-at Authors met at a dinner party.

THE INTERNET is a very handy tool in the mating game should One have extraordinarily unusual sexual tastes or an extraordinarily unusual appearance. It allows One to get straight to the point. Let's face it, any One browsing skinnywrigglymingebags.com knows exactly what they're after.

SPEED DATING is an extension on meeting through the Internet in that One has the ability to scroll through a variety of potential mates whilst having the additional advantage of being close enough to smell them.

ACROSS A CROWDED ROOM There's nothing like the *frisson* of passion One can achieve when One inexplicably catches a beautiful stranger's eye, although why strangers should be throwing eyeballs at One is something of a mystery. Perhaps it's an attention-seeking thing.

MEETING AT A POPULAR MUSIC CONCERT has advantages in that, in the sweaty, pulsating *mêlée*, One may take the opportunity to indulge in sly bodily contact and try before One buys.

MEETING AT AN ORGY A bit of a dampener on courtship, since it's all deeply unromantic. But, to be sure, it's a lot less stressful.

THE DRINKS PARTY Because they have no formal order to them, no placement and nowhere to sit, drinks parties are nothing like as efficient for mate-meeting as dinner parties. That said, they're still better than *Star Trek* conventions.

STAR TREK CONVENTIONS There is categorically nothing worth meeting and mating with at a *Star Trek* convention.

THE EXECUTION OF A HEAD OF STATE This is one of the hot spots for mate-meeting. Think about it: a large crowd of sweating, impatient, over-excited people, the compulsive, tenebrous beats of the death drums and, at the command 'Fire!', an overwhelming surge of power that causes an explosion of lustful pins and needles to One's extremities.

Courtship that Counts: The next rung up on the lovely ladder of love

Thus, now the scent of desire is in the air, there's a mate caught in the cross-hairs of lust – but how does One take it to the next, more intimate stage?

BEGGING, it has to be said, is reliable but not exactly *Posh*. And should One feel a compulsive urge to throw One's self on One's knees, try not to cry through the nose; it's hard to say yes to a stalactite of snot.

Many modern maters have a lot of time for bespoke ROHYPNOL, which can be made from berries and hedgerow roots foraged from motorway lay-bys.

Communicating One's open willingness through eighteenth-century FAN LANGUAGE or the elegant semaphore of where and how One wears a beauty spot only works with members of the Sealed Knot and lycanthropes.

Desperate maters who've tried the ultra-traditional GUITAR SERENADE below a moonlit balcony technique often find themselves urinated upon.

Then we have the ultra-modern solution of TEXTING One's wanton willingness (not easy if One's predictive text facility is on override or One's button is a little sticky).

Should none of the above produce the desired reaction, explore the charmingly retro habit of DROPPING ONE'S MONOGRAMMED HANDKERCHIEF in a carefully choreographed show of great elegance at the feet of the One whose genitals One wishes to get to know better.

Doing Sex: The act, the aftermath and the after-sales service

Of course, the details, the fantasies, the outfits and the equipment of doing sex are all a matter for personal taste. As, indeed, should be the gender, star sign, age and position on the food chain of the partner in question.

Regardless of how One likes One's friction, there are a variety of occurrences and situations which could cause embarrassment if not handled Poshly.

Here follow some common questions:

Q) *My partner in sex wishes to be tied to the bed post. Is there a proprietary knot?*

A) The answer very much depends on whether the bonds in question are silken or hemp. For silk, a competently executed 'monkey fist' is most ornamental, whilst hemp rope responds well to a 'dolly trucker hitch'.

Q) *Spit or swallow?*

A) One should never speak with One's mouth full, so the answer is obvious.

Q) *How may I say 'no' without causing offence?*

A) Tact dictates the onus is on the refuser to make themselves in the future so unattractive they are never asked to do sex again and therefore never in the difficult position of stating a refusal.

Q) *How may I say 'yes' without sounding desperate?*

A) Swiftly fill your mouth with a part of the sex partner in question thus rendering the desperate 'yes' inaudible through a gag of flesh.

Q) *Having grown up in New York, I've never seen a foreskin; do they bite?*

A) To be foreskinned is to be forearmed in this case. Foreskins provide a decorative frill to the very end of a gentleman's finery and so, as such, there is little risk of being bitten. (Do, however, watch out for entanglement.)

Q) *I have long been disappointed in my desire to be Vagitarian. Any suggestions?*

A) There are many books on Lesbianage that can be consulted. Try *Taking it on the Chin, My Life* by Ursula Mannish, Duchess of Quimbledon, which provides hints, tips and diagrams.

Q) *My partner in sex wishes us to involve other people in our fun. Are formal introductions necessary?*

A) Well, if One has a hand free to shake with, it is only polite.

Q) *My partner in sex is so good at doing sex that the act itself takes no more than seconds. Is there a competitive event or tournament they could enter?*

A) Yes.

Q) *How may condoms, their purpose fulfilled, be discreetly disposed of?*

A) Subterfuge and sleight of hand (or, indeed, sleight of mouth, in some cases) are a considerable boon in this situation. Gingerly remove the object in question (guard against spillage), tie it off, then use basic balloon-bending techniques to knot a Staffordshire flatback figurine which may be hidden within a display of china ornaments until One can get to a bin.

Q) *Should One ever own up to a wet patch?*

A) Poshness dictates that any wet patches, spillages, seepages or slicks that have inadvertently occurred should be gallantly covered in the manner of Sir Walter Raleigh's cloak. Although, if One finds One's self without a cloak (what with One being entirely naked and all), a hood will do.

Q) *I have been told by previous partners in sex (and indeed by a few taxi drivers) that my personal configuration is prone to the production of loud 'booming' noises whilst in the midst of grownup fun. What may I do?*

A) This is not as unusual a problem as One may at first think. The insertion of a knitwear baffle or, better still, a custom-made wind sock will mean an end to the embarrassment.

Q) *I am desperate to do sex with some One or something. In fact, I really don't mind paying for it. Where may I go?*

A) There are most marvellous places for those as you who are more than prepared to cross the odd palm with coinage for executive relief. Consult a local telephone directory under 'Muffaterias'.

Q) *I am monstrously good-looking. What may I do?*

A) See Oneanism, page 195.

The morning after the knight before: Chivalry in the face of dog breath

After a night spent squelching, panting and subjecting the bedclothes to a carnal spin cycle, how does life look in the morning? Does rosy-fingered dawn bring a golden glow of honeyed love or steel-grey shards of remorse, regret and flaccid embarrassment?

One thing is for sure, with the benefit of daylight and without that soft-focus pink nimbus that alcohol in quantity provides, everything appears very different. Things look longer, looser, puckered and shadowed by grey. What felt like sexy peach-down the previous evening is exposed as loosely curled upper-lip hair. What appeared to be a majestically rigid sceptre of ridged passion obviously has a day job as a loose association of barely joined, semi-filled pockets of wrinkled skin garnished with the gingeriest of ginger pubic hair which, in candle-light, looked such a rich, mouth-watering auburn.

If the rumpled, badly organised cold buffet of fleshy leftovers before One weren't enough, there's the following to remember:

To dodge dog breath, breathe as inconspicuously as possible through the mouth, keeping the nostrils closed and the head averted whilst the eyes are thrown casually (and rather painfully) back towards One's partner in sex. A courteous lover will also talk out of the side of the mouth, like Popeye, to divert the stream of One's own halitosis.

To say it with flowers: Rosemary means remembrance, poppies mean forget it, soapwort suggests a clean slate whilst sphagnum moss is really rather self-explanatory.

To avoid discomfort when meeting casual partners in sex on the street, feign a recent stroke.

To discreetly suggest that the experience enjoyed needs paying for, start a charmingly whimsical but nevertheless pepperish conversation about values: 'How much do you think One paid for that lovely mirror?' ... 'Do guess how expensive those ravishing Murano wall sconces were' ... 'I bet no one could begin to put a value on that charming garniture'; and then, 'If money *were* to change hands, how high would One value what happened all over your sweating body last night?' Then simply produce an invoice for the exact amount suggested.

A checklist for gentlemen

Now that the deed (and, indeed, all the fun) is done, a gentleman should most assiduously demonstrate that, far from 'wham bam, thank you, ma'am' and wiping it on the curtains on the way out, One does indeed show *respect* in the morning. The perfect expression of that very respect would be to:

* Suggest a second crack (at it)
* Swap business cards
* Leave a tip (a gentleman should never be seen untipped)
* Enquire fairly and firmly about the missing wrist watch
* And, indeed, signet ring and silver-topped walking cane
* Make tea
* Offer to wipe up the worst

Discreet clinics

An occasional consequence of doing sex is unwell mating equipment. However, an urgent word of warning: before committing One's self to a hospital visit, make sure that the unpleasant state the piece of mating equipment has assumed is not the habitual state of mating equipment after a heavy night. Give it a thorough going-over with a damp chamois leather and, if it looks no better, then take it to a discreet clinic. These are places with large brass signs outside on which are copperplate-engraved words like 'urinary', 'urethro' and 'renal', all to make it sound as if it's weeing that's brought the problem on, not doing sex.

Reproduction: A cuntclusion

Whoever came up with the extremely good idea of making doing sex so very much fun deserves a pat on the back (or, indeed, the front, if they prefer it).

Humans – silly creatures, by and large – went out of their way to make the simple act of intimate friction much more complicated than it need be. So, it's up to the Posh to set a thoroughly good example and to show (sometimes even in public) when downstairs fun needs a flourish or two.

Of course, for the majority of humankind doing sex is just the means to a very particular end. After all, it's not just about the mingling of hot juices – there's what happens to DNA once it's stirred up to a salty froth and left to bake at womb temperature for nine months . . .

CHAPTER NINE

One's Evolution

Dynasties and Dyniceties

It is so frightfully dull finding One's self part of somebody else's dynasty. Whenever possible, One should work hard to start One's own. After all, it's nice to leave something for the children after One goes, and a dynasty is a perfect and very thoughtful post-mortem gift for One's offspring.

Starting a dynasty from scratch may seem somewhat daunting at first, but the bottom-line basics for dynastic success (the provision of children, an unusual name and a high degree of personal lustre) aren't outstandingly hard to achieve. There are the traditional extras associated with the top-of-the range dynasties, such as habitual incest, matricide, fratricide, catricide and unusual or binary chromosome count, but these can come later. In fact, just try to stop them.

The simple, straightforward naming of an heir or an heiress is all One needs to get the ball rolling. Clever dynasts will plan the origination of off-spring meticulously to ensure that the fruit of their loins is to be the veritable cherry on top of the fruit salad of society. So, they'll go to considerable lengths to mingle fluids with the fluids of a One who has aptitudes and abilities of the physical extremities they themselves lack. This is so terribly important; the moribund spectre of today's upper classes must act as an example to all what can go wrong when breeding habits become sloppy.

Therefore, successful dynasts should never forget that One has an opportunity to ensure that One's offspring are a lot lovelier and better looking than anything bred before. In fact, it's not so much an opportunity as a responsibility really. After all, it's about good breeding (literally), setting an example (wondrously) and populating the planet with myriad little Ones until doomsday comes (*Poshly*).

Some dynasties One might have heard of

It's always worthwhile having a look around at the strengths and weaknesses of other dynasties for inspiration. Here are a few:

The Medici	Inspired the artistic sort to invent the Renaissance and greetings cards
The Borgias	Ruthless, toothless and very good in bed
The Windsors	A dynasty on a scale rather at odds with their large homes
The Colbys	More royal than the Windsors but less reliable in a crisis
The Vanderbilts	Like the above, only real
The Ming Dynasty	Named after the noise their pots made when fingered
The Kennedys	A large collection of boisterously healthy Irish Americans with the worst sort of luck
The Caesars	Did not invent the Caesar Salad. That was Caesar Ritz (who was actually far *Posher*)
The Bourbons	The best the French could come up with
The Napoleons	The second best the French could come up with
The Ptolemaic Dynasty	Should get a prize for their imaginative use of 'P' and a special prize for incest, which they did so very well

What One's chromosomes cay about One: Or, the ins and outs of good husbandry

There are neither hard nor fast rules for breeding. It is, by its very nature, a relative issue (particularly for the Ancient Egyptians and those from New Zealand). The principle is straightforward and should be seen, at its most simplistic, as a jolly good game of noughts and crosses. For every weak spot (or nought), find a partner who can offer the opposite in abundance (a cross). Thus, eventually, One will cancel out the other until something akin to a God-like state is achieved.

So, for those with a profile prone to chinlessness: find a breeding partner with a chin like a cross-country locomotive at full tilt. People with short, bandy lower limbs should seek to mate with gazelle-legged partners, in the same way that people prone to corpulence can re-balance their genetic legacy by mingling their chubby DNA with sex fellows of ballerina-like willowiness. Basically, where one partner goes 'in', the other should go 'out' so that, as a breeding pair, One's DNA and indeed One's physicality should fit together like adjoining pieces on a jigsaw. And, then, the offspring, abundant and with folds of healthy milk-sodden flesh gleaming pink and pearly, may be exhibited for the admiration of others.

Off-the-shelf progeny: A convenience or a curse?

If One conceives a white-hot compulsion to mate with quite the wrong sort and One is of a considered and responsible conscience, then it's natural and appropriate to do sex, but not to mate. Thus, in One's state of socially responsible, self-enforced barrenness, One can explore the techniques available to provide offspring using the DNA of others.

SURROGACY is at the heart of most Greek tragedies. More often than not, some god or other transforms itself into an item of intimate feminine application simply so they may impregnate a specifically comfy nymph, who then ends up giving birth to a bizarre creature, half God/half highly compacted cotton wool with a loop of cotton for a head and skin that feels like a dry-weave top sheet. Or wings. These days, surrogacy can be done in the comfort of One's home. Simply purchase the reproductive element One lacks, be it egg or seed, hire a womb like a lock-up-garage, and sit back until it cooks.

TEST-TUBE PREGNANCIES Growing babies scientifically is fascinating, but heaven knows what e-numbers they contain.

THE DICKENSIAN ART OF ADOPTION should really be more popular. Simply bowl into one of the meaner cottages lived in by One's most lowly estate workers (do, however, check they're attractive and reasonably symmetrical under all that dirt) and swoop up One of their many offspring so that it may be brought up as one of One's own. That simple.

ADOPTING AN ABROAD CHILD takes time and requires plenty of paperwork, but it's worth it since, in Abroad, they often have far too many children they don't know what to do with. In fact, Hollywood premieres these days are replete with A-list actresses at the head of a flotilla of exotically attired Abroad children whom they have either adopted or been given as a present by their agent.

Splendidly blended: Becoming an evil step

By far the best use of One's time, if all the above fails to suit, is to marry a dynasty-in-waiting. Elderly or rather frail single parents with a bevy of healthy, attractive children are often considered to be the more popular catches on the marriage market.

The art of being a step-parent fell somewhat into decline in the twentieth century but is now back with a bang. The secret is simple, in that there's no One who expects a step-parent to be nice so, by and large, don't be. Then, every now and again, be a little bit nice, which the step-children will mistake for love.

If all else fails, there are always the old-fashioned ways to fall back on.

Growing children One's self in nine easy steps

Obviously, doing sex is involved, but once that's all done and dusted (or, more accurately, wiped), then Madame Nature takes over.

STEP ONE: CROSSING THE THIN BLUE LINE. Now One's got a cute little pink tadpole inside One, One has to give up loads of things, like smoking, drinking, soft cheese, jousting, a sense of humour and, most important of all, patience.

STEP TWO: LINE YOUR FAVOURITE HANDBAG WITH CLING FILM because, by thunder, you'll be being sick a lot. Hurling delicately and in a civilised manner needs practice.

STEP THREE: DON'T RESIST BUT EMBRACE ONE'S STRETCH MARKS. Encourage them to form elegant patterns based on Georgian damasks. Or, for the truly fine-skinned, take time to encourage them to form One's full coat of arms.

STEP FOUR: FOOD CRAVINGS IN PREGNANCY are, believe it or not, where most nutritionists get their best ideas from. Let's face it, only some

One pregnant would suggest half of what Heston Blumenthal serves up. Heston, by the way, is the proud mom of five-year-olds, Veronica and Celeriac.

STEP FIVE: NOW THE BUMP IS GETTING NICE AND BIG ensure you never go anywhere in public without at least five other females in an identical condition. Move slowly and deliberately, puffing and burping like a herd of vegiverous dinosaurs.

STEP SIX: TRY AND REMEMBER what One's feet look like

STEP SEVEN: TRY AND REMEMBER what it was like to get to the loo in time

STEP EIGHT: HAVE A BABY. The easy bit, really, since there's nothing any One can do to stop it. Why, the force of gravity alone is enough to ensure the baby's going to find itself propelled towards the light, and that's without even considering contractions ... No, having a baby is easy; it's having a baby in such a way that it doesn't bring fistfuls of a lady's internal person with it that's the tricky part (and ensuring that the little blighter doesn't rush so quickly through the turnstile it creates a vertical smile from 'ere to 'ere). But then, that's more or less why nearly all drugs were invented, particularly the mind-washing ones that cleanse the brain of all the pain birth lays on just in time to get pregnant again.

Which is why many opt for:

STEP NINE: TOO POSH TO PUSH. Many in the medical profession rather prefer to remove babies through special holes they make because they feel there's less to go wrong. Many now offer 'packages', in which babies, cellulite, tattoos and back hairs are removed all at once.

Babies: What Are They All About?

Babies are designed to look and smell cuter than fresh-baked biscuits. This is to make up for their unbelievably selfish behaviour, filthy temper and inability to help out around the house. On the upside, when they're not aggressively, impatiently pissed off with something, they can be watched like television.

Choosing baby names

Choosing baby names is difficult but not insurmountable. Being in charge of a baby, requires all sorts of decisions on which One simply can't ask the little blighter's opinion. So, One just gets on with it and authorises that circumcision, sacks that wet nurse, simply *insists* on swaddling or, indeed, names the baby Gandalf, Frodo or George W.

Since society finds making its mind up harder and harder, modern babies have names long enough to constitute a list of the surnames of a Sportistic team. Indeed, there are some who call their babies exactly that. But what One really should bear in mind is that One pays by the letter for engraving or monogramming, so twelve initials will make for expensive pillowcases and silver salad servers. Besides, twelve initials would create a monogram of intense and annoying floridity.

When naming, do try to steer clear of obvious *double entendres*:

Martha Farquhar
Mac Hunt
Ophelia Balls
Heidi Sikh
Norbert Dentressangle

Or initials that create inappropriate monograms:

Nathan Oliver Barret
Barbara Umbrella Mason
Simon Martin Edward Grigson
Fellatia-Louise Amy Nuella Jejune

Naming the child after the place in which it was conceived is really far too much information. And giving the baby a name to live up to, like Temperance Charity Liberance or Jesus, is really not very kind. Then there's modern society's abysmal lack of general knowledge and lack of any kind of classical education, which means few know what names actually mean, which perhaps goes far to explain why the young of our world look so perpetually disenfranchised beneath their cottony cowled hoods.

So, as a civilising act of globally shared knowledge, here follow some of our society's most common names, explained so that those about to be in charge of a baby know exactly what that very baby has to live up to.

Boys	Girls
Adolf – a very tough name to live up to	**Asia** – parents on the run from the law
Aubrey – not the marrying sort	**Brittany** – ferry
Craig – some sort of cleft	**Dymphna** – neither lovely in person nor personality
Evelyn – 'it takes all sorts'	**Evelyn** – 'it takes all sorts of sorts'
Florian – a lovely name for a café	**Joanna** – rhyming slang for piano
Godric – unusually sleeved	**Mandy** – hardy
Ken – polari for Kenneth	**Melanie** – a melodious sort of name
Laurence – he who is to be always bossed around by women	**Mia** – mean parents who pay by the letter
Leonard – always preceded by Mr as in, 'Your client's ready for rinsing, Mr Leonard'	**Moon** – more than a bit hippy. Will grow to have a large bottom
Oliver – sporty	**Niamh** – daughter of dyslexia, Queen of Connemara
Roddy – 'not quite right'	**Olivia** – one who tastes of olives
Ringo – a bouncy sort of name	**Philippa** – lover of horses (bizarrely)
Rudolf – 'not quite right and erratically German with it'	**Saffron** – born yellow
Sebastian – floppy	**Saskia** – from the Greek for 'pretentious'
Tony – foppy	**Xanthe** – she who is born to commune-dwelling, tree-living-performance-arting parents

Failsafe Posh names: The top ten

Rank	Girls	Boys
10	Lettice	Pan
9	Artemis	Wat (as in Tyler)
8	Margaret	Cagney (as in James = boys, as in Lacey = girls)
7	Interflora (this one carries with it a potential endorsement deal)	Akhenaton
6	Sweetie	Justinian
5	Delilah (something of a Posh role model)	Quentin (but only for the fifth)
4	Juno	Wart
3	George (very smart and rather Bloomsbury)	Lucifer
2	Britannia	Capability (as in Brown)
1	Dolly (after Parton)	Rex (self-explanatory)

Nicked names: Shortenings

A Posh name rolls so deliciously off the tongue, it really is a terrible shame to chop it up into bite-size pieces all so that the inelegant and uneducated can speak it. Names carry rhythms and also magic. For Pagans and, indeed, some other exquisitely fanciful pre-Christian peoples, using some One's full name carried power with it.

The generation of familiar names that don't even have the slender legitimacy of being a shortening but are derived from a physical peculiarity or propensity really mustn't be tolerated outside the nursery. People who yacht are the worst. They're forever calling each other ridiculous things like 'Tig', 'Frogger', 'Floppy', 'Limpet' and 'Vadj'.

Generally speaking, additions to names, such as 'Junior' or 'the younger' (as in Pitt), and numbers, such as 'the third' (as in George) or 'the fourth' (as in George Hamilton), or 'the fifth, sixth, seventh and eighth' (as in George Foreman), should be used sparingly. Although it does help tell the little blighters apart.

There are also, amongst the upper-classish sort, those who have names that have been specifically designed so that only other upper-classish sorts know how they are pronounced. This is all intensely annoying and really rather pleased with itself and makes every One think that these people should simply start again with something much more straightforward. Some of the worst are:

* Beauchamp (pronounced Beecham)
* Cholmondley (pronounced Chumley)
* Exoskeleton (pronounced Eston)
* Battingaverage (pronounced Barrat)
* Grosvenor (pronounced Grovnor)
* Skittlewick (pronounced Tent-flap)
* Genitalpiercing (pronounced Gwyneth Paltrow)

Children

Children are what happens after babies and, in many respects, they're no improvement. They are theoretically designed to be angelically endearing and so One has to approach children with an extremely patient demeanour and be ready to interpret every single selfish, impertinent, destructive and wilful thing they do or say *as* angelically endearing.

They're also rubbish at keeping secrets and a real liability in social situations, where they'll go out of their way to say the one thing everybody else is thinking about an unfortunate-looking person but wouldn't dream of saying out loud.

Techniques for training children (also works adequately well on household pets)

There's an enormous amount of tosh spoken about 'spoiling' children. The British, in particular, live in morbid dread of giving their children too many presents or loving them too much. This, coupled with the fact that British children live in cold, creeping dread of being sent away to school, means they tend to be very whey-faced. And they jump a mile at loud bangs. Growing up 'without' seems to do just as much harm as growing up 'with'. American children, on the other hand, are indulged so much (particularly with food) that they rarely have time or enough space in their mouths to say 'please' to One, or to thank One. So, what is the best course of action when it comes to training children?

If denial makes children nervy and indulgence makes children complacent, then logic would suggest an approach that combines the best of both. It has long been recognised that One may very efficiently spoil children out of being spoilt. One can, as it were, take the little dears fully around the 365 degrees of spoildom so that spoliation has no meaning. By the time One's progeny own everything there is to own and use the Ritz the way other children use fast-food chains, all that's left for them to wish for is World Peace.

However, to counteract the risk of *über*-spoildom and to ensure the little cherubs don't become unmannered in the American fashion – tease them mercilessly. One should, of course, buy One's children their heart's desire but, rather than just giving it to them over the breakfast table as if it had no value and had been bought at no effort, squeeze every last drop of psycho-drama from the situation. Make the little Ones cry, no, *weep*, from the gratitude of it all by slowly ratcheting the emotional dial up beyond the red danger zone until their bubbling tide of thanks and love reaches a pitch of emotional eloquence far, far beyond the value of the coveted object.

Although text-book good manners or Correct Form is so odiously condescending in grown-ups, it is essential in children and household pets. They rarely have anything to say for themselves, are only occasionally amusing and spend more time taking than giving, so it's of paramount importance they do so with polish.

Children are also as annoyingly prone to ailments as pets. And when either is unwell, there is no pretence at bravery or a stiff upper lip. Ill children, who depend on being able to run around a lot, have nothing with which to fill their days apart from moaning. They also feel that unless sweatily and uncomfortably stuck, limpet-like, to an extremity of their parents at all times, they're not doing their job properly.

Digestive complaints are common, since the little bleeders love eating out of bins and licking things. Slightly older children love having digestive complaints which allow them the pleasure of moaning loudly from the loo and then, horror of horrors, asking to be 'wiped'.

Colds and upper respiratory complications give One's progeny the opportunity to cultivate mucus by the gallon. Child mucus seeps, boils and bubbles to the surface like magma through any available fissure or orifice. Children are great at snot stalactites.

Skin embarrassments, verrucas, warts or scabs are particularly popular, since they may be poked, prodded and, if the child is nimble enough, nibbled off. Children love itching, picking and chewing at themselves.

Having nits is one thing, but having nits *Poshly* requires a lot of effort. Luckily for the nit-ee, history can help. Throughout the eighteenth century, persons of fashion, out of a philanthropic sense of sentimentality for lower life forms, allowed their beautiful perukes to become guesthouses for all of creepy-crawly-dom, thereby inspiring the artful silversmiths of the day to create the most fancifully elegant implements with which to scratch. An outbreak of nits at school may be successfully and glamorously treated with a liberal dosing of eighteenth-century rococo head-itchers. If all else fails, lock the infectee outside and hand them over to One's outdoor staff for a vigorous application of pesticide.

How to break children in using simple equestrian and dog-handling techniques

* For boisterous boys, a few dozen laps of an indoor riding ring on the end of a medium-length lunge rein will soon bear fruit.
* To stop children getting lonely and fractious when left out in a field for months on end, buy a donkey.
* When out for a walk, some children tend to lurch forward at the sight of a distant friend, ice-cream van or busy main road. Get into the habit of restraining them by holding back their collar firmly and fairly. If this behaviour continues, let the collar go unexpectedly. The child will eventually give up all desire to lurch.
* Praise children enthusiastically should they do something right, like coming immediately when called, successfully offering up a paw or jumping a five-bar gate without hesitation.

Keeping Children Busy

Time was once that One didn't need to make an effort to keep children busy, since they had habitual playfellows like cholera, plague, diphtheria and childhood prostitution which kept them from under One's feet. Should they have been healthy, there was more than enough to occupy their little minds (and tiny, brittle fingers) over at the mill, down the mine or up the chimney.

But today's child, so swaddled and molly-coddled, expects perpetual diversion: a veritable cold buffet of things to do. Should they not be provided with things to do, they make good their threat to grow up bad.

So, as beneficent, engaged and much-loved parents themselves, our wonderful Authors have provided a list of suggestions to keep the little Ones busy:

* Colouring in (in the high Renaissance manner)
* Building bricks (with a master class in Post-Modernism)
* Playing battleships (with particular reference to Octavian's defeat of Anthony at the battle of Actium, using perfectly accurate but miniaturised replicas)
* Noughts and crosses (using x and y chromosomes within a laboratory environment)
* Origami (high-denomination banknotes look splendid)
* Jigsaws (fifth-century BC mosaic restoration)
* Playing IT (inventing a successor to the Internet)
* Dressing up (the creation of an autumn/winter couture collection)
* Spaniel dressage
* Cat's cradle (with specific reference to the architectural *oeuvre* of Daniel Liebeskind)
* Playing Simon Says (in Ancient Greek)
* Pin the tail on the donkey (elementary veterinary plastic surgery)
* Hide and seek (with One's footman)
* Sleeping lions (with sleeping lions)
* Charades (directed by Tim Burton)

Posh parties for charming children

It's a parental duty of biblical magnitude that One familiarises children with the responsibilities and joys of entertaining as early in their lovely lives as possible. Entertaining is a crucial rite in the sanctity of *Posh* and so children, however young, should be initiated as quickly as possible.

Children's parties must never be dismissed as being mere children's parties. Do not give in. One should not cease in One's efforts to ensure that a party for seven six-year-olds is every bit as stylish, every bit as lovely, every bit as surprising as a drinks party on an Art Deco yacht moored just off some ravishing Adriatic island. No matter how efficiently One's child might whine, no matter how high-pitched their remonstrations, there are some venues One should never, ever consider as an appropriate background for birthday celebrations:

THEME PARKS are breeding grounds of the MRSA virus, e-coli, b-coli, broc-coli, tertiary syphilis and galloping, highly contagious commonness.

BOWLING ALLEYS require One to wear clothes made from man-made materials. Then there are the terrifying shoes they subject One to, plus the humiliation of having to watch them spray disinfectant into the very shoes One was wearing after they are handed back. As if.

FAST-FOOD RESTAURANTS offer an environment in which to celebrate One's child's birthday based quite closely on the seventh circle of hell. With e-numbers.

RESIDENTIAL MORRIS-DANCING COURSES such as might be enjoyed by middle-aged men called Morris aren't good places for children.

ADVENTURE PLAYGROUNDS are actually brightly painted, telegraph-pole-stockaded arenas for social engineering.

THE CIRCUS is to be avoided at all costs for fear of bumping into family members forced to exhibit themselves for money.

Far better is to bedeck some appropriate venue in celebratory bunting and provide for One's offspring the kind of birthday One simply *knows* will catapult the little darling's status in the classroom right to the very top of the primary-school pecking order.

You will need:
* A petting zoo full of highly venomous and/or extremely dangerous endangered species to pet
* An expert in heraldic balloon sculpture so each child may bend their own crest
* Some *haute cuisine* e-numbers invented specially for and named after the birthday boy or girl
* A birthday cake that manages to get close, using spun sugar, to what Antonio Canova managed to achieve in highly polished marble
* A minibus full of soap-opera stars to help pour out the orange squash
* Party hats flown in that morning from Venice
* Crackers flown in that morning from Beijing
* Jelly flown in that morning from the secret jelly mines of Montana
* An internationally acclaimed rap DJ to play pass the parcel
* Going-home bags from Tiffany
* A nip or two of vodka for the orange squash when every One gets a little too energetic
* A social secretary to deal with the thank-you cards

Children's entertainers: Pinning the exclusion order on the paedophile — Fun for all ages

Can you spot the paedo? Simply cut around the exclusion order and pin it, using a drawing pin, through the forehead of the children's entertainer who looks the most suspicious.

Children's Pets

Pets were invented to teach children all there is to know about mortality. Since no child worth their name would ever take responsibility for bathing a pet, feeding a pet, watering a pet, cleaning out its cage or taking it to the vet, all that's left for the child to get their teeth into is grieving for a pet.

Bearing in mind that animals have evolved their own techniques for measuring how old they are – dog years, cat years, budgie months, hamster minutes – it is inevitable that the Grim Reaper of the fluffy bunny kingdom will be making hutch-calls on a reasonably regular basis throughout childhood. The debate as a ℘osh parent is whether to do the decent thing and work conscientiously with the bereaved child to get them to understand that the circle of life is an inevitability which should inspire all sentient creatures to seize the day, or whether to sneak to the pet shop to replace the lifeless pet with its doppelgänger. The latter solution, whilst heavy on the logistics (and, it has to be said, luck) is so very much easier on the psyche.

A few tips on nocturnal pet disposal

* Most importantly, make sure the pet is dead. The flat back of a coal shovel should do
* Dig a deep enough hole. It is of paramount importance that the creature be left to decompose in peace without the risk of being dug up by foxes or, indeed, the bereaved child whilst making mud pies
* Forewarn the neighbours. In rural areas, the sight of a shifty figure with a lantern, shovel and potato sack full of something lifeless may very well be a good enough reason to let the dogs out
* Compose a firmly worded justification for the clandestine act for use when the bereaved child eventually finds out (probably in their early thirties) what has actually happened to Ginger
* Never try to flush anything but small fish; there's nothing worse than a gerbil stuck in the U-bend, as any plumber will attest
* Don't bother briefing a florist and on no condition take out a newspaper announcement in the 'Deaths' column
* Whatever happens, ignore the impulse to float the dead creature out into the midst of the moonlit fishpond during an appropriate crescendo from Wagner's Götterdämmerung, while flinging paper aeroplanes which One has set alight at the merrily bobbing corpse

School

Sending a child to school so that they may be educated eventually to be a useful and appropriate member of society is really far less important than simply getting them out of the house.

Posh prep v getting away with not paying

Taking One's child, an innocent, trusting, loving bundle of cells with sweet-tasting earlobes and a perma-smell of pastry and dumping them into a school means their little lives will never be the same again. From being the very centre of family gravity to being but one oik amongst many is rarely a smooth transition for the little cherubim. And then there is the forceful backwash of guilt following on from the waves of relief any parent feels at having escaped the bonds of pre-school slavery. None of it helps. So, it is not a surprise that, over thousands of years, parents have evolved for themselves a belief system that supposes school to be a very good thing indeed and the very thing that will be the making of their child. But, quite frankly, who are they kidding?

In some societies (such as the upper reaches of the British upper classes), a 'good' (i.e. 'expensive') education was considered preferable to being loved. Parents saw a very straightforward fiscal arrangement in paying hundreds of thousands of pounds over a period of eighteen or so years to receive back, at the end of it, a perfectly perfected child who could just get on with its own life without any further call on the parent in question. This, of course, also meant whatever dysfunction they carried with them (homosexuability, sado-masochism, dandruff or socialism) could be blamed on the school, not on the parent. It's a system that has been proved really rather faulty.

It's far better to love One's children (which is free). Lavish attention on them, introduce them to glamour and all that is loveliness at a very early age, then keep a closely indulgent but reasonably relaxed eye on all the growing-up that happens next. Tap them slightly to the left or to the right should they show any signs of wobbling off the path of *Posh*. But, fundamentally, allow them space. In fact, give them their own wing.

With this philosophy in mind, the best school for One's child should be a happy place the little One enjoys going to and in which the little One receives all the nourishment needed to become a bigger One. Which of course means that provided One is prepared to work hard at being a parent, One needn't bankrupt One's self paying others to bring One's children up for One when there are more than a few schools which are free.

Can *Adolescents* Ever *Really* be *Posh*?

It's not just the spots, the greasy hair, the comically large hands with revoltingly sweaty palms; it's not just the sulks, the tantrums, the unwashed socks, the disobedience, the sebum (in gallons), the bedsheets with inexplicable stiff patches, the uncontrollable voice that slides between octaves in an instant and, above all, the nihilism. No, the problem with adolescence is the very musty-smelling entity itself – which is probably why former societies imprisoned their adolescents in convents, monasteries or boarding schools.

To be honest, once adolescence has taken hold, there's really little One can do but wait. Ensuring the afflicted young person has access to all imaginable grooming products sometimes inspires a bit of casual washing. But, fundamentally, be prepared to be repulsed for as long as it takes.

Posh sex education

Should One be able to persuade the adolescent in question to stop doing sex with themselves and start considering doing it with another, chinks start appearing in their shiny, oily, malodorous crust of adolescent armour. The realisation dawns loud and clear that 'another' will need to be attracted, and a plentiful crop of back zits just won't cut the mustard.

A smart, Posh parent will introduce the concept of mating as early as possible in adolescence. But, be warned, nothing makes a stroppy teenager shy like a nervy gazelle more than a parent oozing condescension and sexual informality. No, since adolescents are, by and large, really very stupid (all their brain cells get requisitioned for the purposes of righteous indignation), they're unlikely to question how the sex manuals with explicit pencil drawings, or the condoms, the spot preparations and depilatory creams found their way into their bedroom. No, they'll just get on with it.

Sexual orientation for teenagers: The slippery slope

The downside of getting the adolescent in question to look beyond self-pollution as a full-time career and start sharing fluids with another is that adolescents by their very nature find absolutely *everything* sexually attractive. It takes a good few years of dedicated practice for them to learn how to steer private parts in the right direction without them going off in One's face or letting loose an embarrassing bout of friendly fire.

So, as a parent, patience becomes One's constant companion and perpetual support. The adolescent themselves will eventually put a foot in a camp, and at that point they'll need a Posh parent by their side to help arrange the paperwork and provide invaluable advice on specialist equipment.

Dolly and Rex, a cautionary tale

As an invaluable aid, behold the following. More valuable than the most pompous and expensive of educations, what follows has been designed to be left casually within reach of an impressionable child who would be powerless to resist the impulse to colour it in and, in doing so, learn something.

Behold Dolly and Rex, are they not wonderful children?

See how their shoes shine, see how their hair shines and see them smile.

Dolly and Rex are loved by all.
Dolly and Rex get *all* the attention.

This is Jack. He is ugly on the inside and ugly on the outside. He is wearing brown shoes with blue shorts and is under-groomed. Jack gets no attention. Nobody likes Jack. Jack likes nobody. Jack thinks fourteenth-century Florentine art is tosh. We think Jack is tosh. Don't we?

Jack sees Dolly and Rex. He sees they get *all* the attention. He hates them. He wants to make them ugly like him.

Jack picks up some mud.
Jack throws mud at Dolly and Rex.

But behold. Before the mud hits Dolly and Rex, an angel of incandescent beauty and fierce symmetry appears and deflects the thrown mud back towards the furious Jack.

Then Jack is dragged by his malodorous and unpleasantly cropped hair down into hell where his fingers are stripped off by demons wielding red hot nail scissors and his ear lobes are cut with paper for ever. And ever. Amen.

So, remember: do not throw mud at lovely people. Be lovely instead.

CHAPTER TEN

One's
Termination

Posh Death

Dying gives One a last-ditch (indeed, the very last ditch before One enters One's own freshly dug ditch) opportunity to orchestrate a lovely experience for all concerned. If possible, try to avoid scheduling One's death during the first three weeks of January, a period affectionately known by more jocund funeral directors as 'chucking-out time at the hospice'. The first twenty days or so of every New Year always boast a bottleneck of morbidity, as the terminally unhealthy who have striven hard to make it to Christmas all pass their 'live by' dates at once. That final effort to live longer than the turkey leftovers, combined with the inevitable cold snap and a return to ordinary, boring television schedules, proves far too much for tens of thousands. So, should it be within One's power to shuffle or, more accurately, *swan* off One's mortal coil at a time when fewer people are ill, do it. It also improves One's chances of a decent write-up in the papers. In fact, deaths in August practically guarantee fulsome obituaries.

Lovely ideas for facing the final curtain: The death room

If a solitary death is planned (i.e., without grieving relations), then the world is your sepulchral oyster. In fact, since One's room is the very last thing One will be seeing, please feel free to indulge in the dramatic draping of coal-black crêpe, nodding fountains of deep purple ostrich feathers, cascades of weeping lilies and more black pillar candles than a surprise birthday cake for Ozzy Osbourne.

If One is sharing One's death with One's loved Ones, such obviously sombre displays, tinged as they are with a rather grisly sense of camp, may further upset the upset. A more tactful and considerate hand is called for to soothe those whom One will so soon be leaving behind. Go for a bright, fresh, spring-like feel, implying an optimistic sense of new beginning. Crisp white cotton, clean, fresh and peaceful, will do wonders for lifting a moribund complexion (in fact, don't rule out contacting your chosen funeral director for a few pre-mortem postmortem make-up techniques). A simple vase of hedgerow flowers on a windowsill and a discreet twitter of birdsong will allow One's grieving relations to describe One's passing as 'peaceful' and 'what One would have wanted' and to leave them with comforting thoughts of the circle of life, and death being nature's way of recycling.

I want to live forever: Preservation

The late Eva Perón's funeral directors rather thoughtfully started to inject embalming fluid into her veins weeks before she actually died. This left her, after death, soft, bendy and, apparently, just as much fun as in life.

Long-term preservation of the dead should really be a question of aesthetics rather than ethics. La Perón was indisputably lovely, but to what possible purpose One could put the raddled, mustachioed and cryogenically pickled head of the late Walt Disney is beyond imagination. After all, death really must be seen as a marvellous opportunity to wipe One's own slate clean.

Putting One's house in order before One goes: Briefing a florist

It really is a terribly good idea to sit down (should One still be able to sit) with a good florist before D-day. Guarantee the loveliness of the fateful day by providing a long list of favourite blooms and some rough-sketched ideas of wreaths and casket posies. It is a constant surprise how One's grieving relatives, their judgement no doubt giddied by grief, can let One down when it comes to flowers. Even cultivated septuagenarian aesthetes who keep houses in Antibes, the Hamptons and Mayfair have been known, when faced with so crucial a decision, to choose (amidst rictus-fits of sobbing) MY BEST PAL spelt out in brown chrysanthemums.

D-Day dawns: Time for the final words

After a life lived Poshly, One should, by now, know when to stop. In fact, if One finds One has inadvertently offered the most perfect last words days before the end, then the best thing to do is say nothing more until One finally departs, leaving the world with the most perfect last memory.

Although death can be a rather unsettling experience, avoid unseemly beggings, howlings or, worse still, trite sentimental utterances. And, remember: there's nothing wrong with pre-recording One's last words on a small, easily concealed recording device. This, of course, allows One just to get on with the business of expiring, safe in the knowledge that all One needs to do when the death rattle rises from One's lungs is simply press 'play'.

The fitting end to a lovely life well-lived: Fab funerals and wonderful wakes

As discussed, January passings are a nightmare, since all the professionals couldn't be busier, and you can forget December altogether if you want a good turnout from One's loved ones. So, to avoid disappointment, it's best to book a good few months in advance. On the other hand, funerals in mid-summer never really quite work. For a start, there are too many distractions for mourners, such as holidaying children playing hopscotch in the street, passing ice-cream vans and the inappropriate deafening cheerfulness of summer birdsong. No, mid to late autumn or early to mid spring present the best and most appropriate seasonal backdrops for elegant disposal ceremonies.

It goes without saying that One should keep the talking bits to a minimum. Focus instead on a surprising, diverting but ultimately deeply moving musical programme. It's best to start solemn – Elgar, Beethoven or Black Sabbath; but finish joyous and a bit hopeful – Handel, Mozart or Carly Simon; with something spiritual by, perhaps, Fauré or Neil Diamond in between.

A post-ceremony drinks reception should be the very byword of elegance. After all, there are very few occasions when One can guarantee that all One's friends and family are gathered in elegantly flattering fitted black from head to toe. Although, technically, the darkest navy is much more supportive to the inevitable raw red of the grieving complexion.

Alcohol should be exquisite, bitter and served in near-homeopathic quantities, whilst vol-au-vent cases filled with fish paste well and truly past its sell-by date provides One with a pharaonic opportunity to take a few close friends with One to what must be seen as a Higher drinks party.

Retaining control from beyond the grave: Posh wills, lovely legacies and elegant hauntings

Never forget that having been 100 per cent committed to the credo of Posh in all its lovely forms throughout One's life, death creates an ideal opportunity to try the dark side and go out of One's way to generate the mother of all family feuds.

Face it: even the most carefully wrought and tactful of wills is going to piss off some One or other. So really, why not contrive a series of elegantly evil codicils which require beneficiaries to perform the most extraordinarily capricious acts in One's memory or to affect eccentricities of dress or appearance as a condition of One's postmortem generosity?

If being less than nice to raw-eyed mourners in One's will brings with it a degree of itchy guilt, then an old-fashioned haunting provides a stylishly spectral opportunity to salve the conscience. A Posh manifestation needn't be cosy or too upbeat but, do remember: sigh rather than moan, rustle rather than rattle chains, carry One's severed head like a Hermès clutch bag and, generally speaking, organise One's ectoplasm according to the immutable rule of Poshture (see page 32)

Poltergeist ability should, in fact, be seen as an act of social work (from beyond the grave). Make a point of rearranging the furniture of the living and enjoy hurling their ugly ceramics against the wall. It's an act of kindness they'll thank you for in the end.

Posh ways to die

* Firing squad (insist on being tied to a stake – remember: Poshture)
* Natural causes
* Unnatural acts
* A burst bladder following an unusually long papal coronation
* Knife fight (remember the cutlery rule: start on the outside and work One's way in)
* Guillotining
* An overdose of perming fluid
* An overdose of seminal fluid
* A too-tight tiara
* Blue-blood poisoning
* Being killed whilst killing things
* A surfeit of loveliness
* A dearth of loveliness
* Disembarking (leaving a yacht in Saint Tropez too early)
* Disembowelling (leaving a ski lift in Gstaad too late)
* Politeness
* Impoliteness
* Impropriety
* Piety
* Drowning in a butt of malmsey (or, these days, a very large Pimm)
* Badly hung chandeliers
* Getting morbidly entangled in lace
* Poisonous pigments in wonderful wallpaper
* Spiteful shellfish
* Fatal attraction
* Tailoring
* Noble rot
* Rising damp

Regardless of what happens to the soul after the body, One, satisfied and happy with a life glamorously lived, breathes One's last. Whether choirs of angels, chorus lines of devils or One's illustrious ancestors transformed into fluffy bunnies are there to welcome One to whatever afterlife is *au courant*, the point of a *Posh* life is not where, when or why, but most definitely how.

The Posh Life: One's Final Word

Living life *Poshly* really should be compulsory. For our Authors and their knotless golden brows, *Posh* comes naturally. But, Dear Little Reader, don't be at all put off if you find you have to work at it. No One said the journey through a *Posh* life is an easy stroll through a level landscape of loveliness. All too often, that is the very point to it. It's the effort One expends to get life right that is so very precious. There's a divine energy to it that, once released, returns like a cosmic boomerang, doubled in strength, to illuminate the very corners of the *Posh* soul.

Do nothing effortlessly, unmanneredly or thoughtlessly; strive for glamour on the inside as well as the outside.

In all things be *Posh*.

Index

Acknowledgements

Thank you to any One and anything that's ever borne the name Mitford; to Sophia Topley for '*Negaria*'; to Roger Melly for '*Fuckulent*' and heartfelt thanks to whomever invented gin.

Melanie Milne typed this. Jenny Heller edited, supported, protected and refined this, then Susan Victoria promoted this. Danvers, Gay Dad, Pat Foof and Auntie laughed at this – and so they too all need a really rather stout thanking.